Manipulation, NLP and Body Language Stoicism

The Complete Step-by-Step Guide to Win the War of the Mind and Discover the Dark Secrets of Persuasion and Kamikaze Mind Control

Blake Reyes

© COPYRIGHT 2021 BY BLAKE REYES ALL RIGHTS RESERVED.

This document is geared towards providing exact and reliable information with regards to the topic and issue covered. The publication is sold with the idea that the publisher is not required to render accounting, officially permitted, or otherwise, qualified services. If advice is necessary, legal or professional, a practiced individual in the profession should be ordered.

- From a Declaration of Principles which was accepted and approved equally by a Committee of the American Bar Association and a Committee of Publishers and Associations.

In no way is it legal to reproduce, duplicate, or transmit any part of this document in either electronic means or in printed format. Recording of this publication is strictly prohibited and any storage of this document is not allowed unless with written permission from the publisher. All rights reserved.

The information provided herein is stated to be truthful and consistent, in that any liability, in terms of inattention or otherwise, by any usage or abuse of any policies, processes, or directions contained within is the solitary and utter responsibility of the recipient reader. Under no circumstances will any legal responsibility or blame be held against the publisher for any reparation, damages, or monetary loss due to the information herein, either directly or indirectly.

Respective authors own all copyrights not held by the publisher.

The information herein is offered for informational purposes solely and is universal as so. The presentation of the information is without contract or any type of guarantee assurance.

The trademarks that are used are without any consent, and the publication of the trademark is without permission or backing by the trademark owner. All trademarks and brands within this book are for clarifying purposes only and are the owned by the owners themselves, not affiliated with this document.

TABLE OF CONTENTS

INTRODUCTION **7**
CHAPTER 1 - MIND CONTROL TECHNIQUES **10**
  Mind Control with NLP for Love and Relationships.... 14
  The most Powerful Mind-Power Tool......................... 19
CHAPTER 2 - WHAT'S EMOTIONAL MANIPULATION? .. **22**
  Types of Emotional Manipulation 25
  Behavioral and Character Traits of Manipulators....... 27
CHAPTER 3 - PSYCHOLOGICAL MANIPULATION TECHNIQUES **31**
CHAPTER 4 - THE ROLE OF DEFENCE **36**
  Signs that You're Being Manipulated 36
  Factors that Make You Vulnerable to Manipulation .. 40
  How to Defend Yourself from a Manipulative Person 42
  Practical Tips for Dealing with Predators................... 47
CHAPTER 5 - THE ART OF BODY LANGUAGE **52**
  The Five C's of Body Language................................... 54
  The Subconscious Mind and The Limbic Brain System 62
  The most powerful techniques you can use to fake your body language and manipulate Anyone's 68
CHAPTER 6 - MASTERING THE SECRETS OF NON-VERBAL COMMUNICATION **72**
  How to Interpret Verbal Communication 76
  Verbal and non-verbal communication - what is it 85
  How to Influence and Subdue Anyone's Mind 103

CHAPTER 7 - HOW TO USE SUBLIMINAL MESSAGES TO MANIPULATE 107
CHAPTER 8 - HOW THE EYES CAN TELL US A LOT OF THINGS 113
  The access keys are eye movements 130
CHAPTER 9 - BODY LANGUAGE MISTAKES TO AVOID 141
  Positive Body Language 142
  Negative Body Language 144
  Body Language Mistakes to Avoid 145
CHAPTER 10 - THE ART OF PERSUASION 151
  How to increase our capacity for persuasion 154
  Method of dark persuasion 158
CHAPTER 11 - NEURO-LINGUISTIC PROGRAMMING .. 162
  What is NLP? 162
  Verbal vs. Non-Verbal Communication 165
  Differences between types of communication 175
  5 NLP Techniques You Must Master 200
CHAPTER 12 - STOICISM FOR LIFE 209
  What's Stoicism? 209
  The Most Important Stoic Philosophers 222
  Thinking Like a Stoic 224
  How to Become a Warrior-Philosopher 228
CONCLUSION 232

INTRODUCTION

We'll be exploring a very important topic in this eBook, because of which many people are interested in psychology. This is a type of exploitation that we experience in life all the time. I'm unlikely to be mistaken if I say somebody is constantly trying to manipulate us, and we try to manipulate others as well. And more often than not, we do this unintentionally, intuitively and thus ineptly, because of which our manipulations do not always lead us to the desired result, nor do other people manage to successfully manipulate us. Even so, people accept attempts to constantly manipulate one another. Therefore, understanding that issue is very important. We will explore in this book what coercion is, how it operates, how effective it is and what can and should be done.

Manipulation is a secret psychological tool by which you can compel any person to do the acts you need against his will and interests. But that is the default exploitation description. Let's offer a wider and more practical definition of that talent. Manipulation is a psychological weapon which, like other types of weapons, gives a person the same (and even greater) advantage over other people. You can strike and catch with one arm and you can also protect and defend with it. It helps with survival and success.

A good manipulator, that is, a person who is skillfully in possession of hidden psychological techniques, is far stronger than a person armed to the teeth. Why? Because he can spread the actions he wants to a variety of people and thus solve any problems and activities. And how many problems and tasks can a person armed with a firearm embedded in our understanding solve? Just a couple, right? One weapon's strength has its limitations. But there are no limits to manipulation. Without exception you can manipulate all people, both the most ordinary and the most powerful. Your talents are the only weakness.

The more perfect your skills in manipulation, the more people you can manipulate. There's no limit to the manipulations themselves—you can manipulate any guy. Without exception you can control all men, both the most average and the most powerful and strong. Your talents are the only weakness.

For some, the most terrible thing is people's inability to accept the fact that they are being exploited. If you tell a person that he was a victim of abuse by someone, then he will most likely deny it and continue to do what he has done. Like showing himself and you that his decision is his choice, and no one is controlling them.

As a manipulated person, my conscience, too, doesn't want to admit that I'm being exploited, but I know for sure. My thoughts, decisions, and actions can't be completely clear of others' influence; it's simply impossible to achieve that. And I understand that so to speak, many of my decisions aren't entirely correct, because I make them under the influence of other people coming to me from facts. I don't have to deny that—I have to regulate that.

Those who doubt they are abused deprive themselves of the chance to defend themselves against it. This is the power of manipulation—it affects people not only secretly, but they also don't want to reveal it themselves. If conventional weapons are used, we turn the aggressor into an enemy quickly, and start fighting with him. Yet people don't see the manipulations, they don't want to see, so they follow them obediently. So, think about what power you can achieve if you know how people can be manipulated.

CHAPTER 1

MIND CONTROL TECHNIQUES

Mind control means using the human psychology of one to guide the other person to the conclusion he or she desires. Know these techniques in advance to avoid being fooled by cult groups and illicit traders!

1. Returnability

When a person gives me something such as a gift, praises me, "You're a wonderful person," or helps someone in trouble, I feel the need to respond to it. That is the returning nature.

Usually, a person cannot be favored unilaterally, he must be sure to give something back.

For example, it is the psychology that salespeople use with customers, such as providing bouquets and concert tickets, sending handwritten letters and birthday cards, helping out with the garbage, and holding their shoulders. After that, people who have received benefits are likely to accept solicitations, saying, "The least I can do is to buy a product."

2. Consistency of commitment

With the psychology that you want to do something once and consistently perform actions, or want to be seen by others as consistent, it is very difficult to change what you have decided or promised later.

When you make a decision to do something, of your own choice and without being coerced, you will tell yourself that you can't turn back when you are asked to fulfill it, and more.

3. Authority

Everyone is weak to authority. They tend to follow the instructions of authoritative people without thinking deeply.

Therefore, if you emphasize a relationship with authority or a celebrity who seems to be considered to be authoritative, it is easy to trust the person or organization.

To take advantage of this psychology, dubious associations and bother-to-representatives shoot or show photos with celebrities that represent that they have a good relationship with the person of authority or influence.

4. Low ball

First of all, the solicitation technique started by gently throwing a "low ball" that is easy for the opponent to receive.

If anyone asked you all of a sudden, "Would you like to enroll in religion?" or said "Pay a donation," "Buy this picture," you would refuse immediately.

However, if they said to you, "I'm studying palms," or "Are

you interested in art?" you'd feel more comfortable with them. Those who have been solicited ask themselves "Is it okay to go out with them?" And become more likely to be drawn in.

5. Favor

It is easy for anyone to accept requests from people they like. They also think that they must accept such requests.

Especially for men and women who have romantic feelings, it becomes "naturally answered when asked by someone you like." In that case, the psychology of wanting to be liked by listening to the wishes of the other person also works.

Also, even if you do not think of it at first, you gradually give favor to those who compliment your appearance, sense, work style, or those who feel that your hobbies and outlook on life are suitable. And so, you fall into the same psychological state.

6. If you refuse, concession

With this technique, at first, the person poses an excessive request on the premise that the other party rejects it. At the time it is rejected, concessions are calculated as expected, and the other party is likely to accept the switch to smaller requests easily.

7. Social proof

The psychology of making decisions based on what others think is right, and what they choose, whether or not things are right.

Even if you are not an expert in the field, when you hear that someone around you or a celebrity chooses it, it feels correct and wonderful, and this acts as a powerful judgment.

Therefore, disseminating the story that "a particular entertainer XX selects and uses it" will result in a very high advertising effect.

8. Rarity

The harder it is to obtain, the more valuable the opportunity given to you to obtain it.

"Limited 100 pieces only," and "Now only" gifts are good examples of this technique.

Recruiting cults and the like go one step further with phrases like, "You are one of tens of thousands of people selected," "You are lucky." They skillfully tackle the psychology of the other person.

9. Perception of Contra strike

Human perception and cognition have a large contrasting effect when subjected to contrasting stimuli.

For example, if you show a cheap item immediately after you show an expensive item, people will see it cheaper than it really is.

Another example of applying this mechanism; A person drives an invitee into a desperate psychological state by showing a video that radically edits unfortunate events in the world such as war, disaster, and crime. Immediately afterward, he solicits, saying, "Only the truth taught by the gurus will save you."

10. Fear

It is a common practice of cults to stir up the other person's fear.

Also, those who offer a defection repeatedly show an example of people that became unhappy because they lacked that defection. In that case, not only the person himself, but also his family and descendants, or even the ancestors of that world, become more unhappy, and the effect is further enhanced.

Mind Control with NLP for Love and Relationships

In a relationship, a word said unconsciously or with conviction can be worth more than a thousand images. For example, the belief that "men always leave me" leads to an experience that turns that idea into truth, so that in the end men leave you, cheat on you, or want to go to bed and nothing else.

Those words that come from the drawer of advice and proposals of love and desire are mental schemes that help to disturb or improve relationships, from the most intimate, without consciously noticing it. 'Intuitive Intelligence' is a way of interpreting the purpose of NLP, which is defined in what the acronym describes: Neurolinguistic programming, the dynamics between the mind (neuro) and language (linguistic) and how the relationship between the two affects the body and behavior (programming). FUCSIA magazine proposed the application of Neurolinguistic Programming in couple relationships to the greatest expert on the subject.

1. What is NLP?

Neurolinguistic Programming (NLP) is the study of the structure of subjective experience and what we can calculate from it. It is a model that goes beyond the obvious and helps us make better decisions according to our objectives. But it is a subjective model. We will discuss more of this in this book.

2. And what is that subjectivity?

Our beliefs, what we know and believe to be true. NLP helps us to know how our mind works, how we communicate and behave. Everything we see, feel, and hear is veiled by our subjectivity.

3. Can NLP techniques be applied in pairs?

Yes, NLP makes evident to us the resources we have within ourselves to relate to in any field, obviously including the couple relationship. When we relate to others, we encounter two different realities, two different belief structures, knowledge, information, physiology, and development. In relationships, it helps create harmony and install positive state mechanisms in our minds, what in NLP we call 'anchors.' It leads us to focus on what we want.

4. Do these 'anchors' produce states of pleasure?

The anchor is a neuro-association between an intense internal state (emotion) and an external stimulus (touch, see, hear). Also, the place, the aromas, the environment, the objects are anchors. So, if you consciously create anchors between the two, you can stimulate the intense desire to be together.

5. In other words, subliminal techniques with the partner?

In NLP, we do not use subliminal messages, and we direct the unconscious mind to start generating the results it wants. But, only you and no one but you decide to change.

6. So, do the parameters of 'good sex' and the orgasm quest change?

Perhaps all humans act on those parameters. The parameters are created by who? Has there ever been a time when you have intensely enjoyed being with your partner, and it has been more fabulous than an orgasm? Surely yes! But what makes us believe that "it must be" clouds these beautiful experiences. Again, we return to beliefs, and for this, it would be good to answer yourself: what beliefs do I have that are mine? Have they been useful to me? What do I believe now of many subjects I have questioned myself?

7. How to use anchors in the sexual game?

When you feel extremely good, so much that your heart is pounding and you are enjoying it to the fullest... in the most exciting moment of the experience, say something in your mind! Project an image into your mind. Do something now, and your brain will create a connection, a neural network with this state that will be increasingly pleasant. So, the two in unison will begin to create mind maps that generate full understanding and vital focus.

8. Does love count in NLP mind maps? Is there a technique to fall in love?

Love is not had, and it is not a thing; it is a state that you create and decide to live. In the brain, in the neural connection, every thought is translated into a chemical that generates emotions. If your brain is loaded with the 'love chemical,' let's put it that way, everything that person says, everything they do is perfect.

9. Why is it that sometimes, what is said and what is desired does not flow in the relationship?

The apparent contradiction happens because we do not realize what the other is saying to us with his body. So we do not listen to the body, the tone of voice, the looks and the gestures, and although the information is there, we become blind.

10. Would NLP apply to sex therapy interventions?

A lot of sexual problems between couples are the expectations created by the environment of what should or should not be; of what is satisfactory or not; of taboos, the bad, the accepted, the not accepted. Couples come into the relationship littered with so much trash that it doesn't allow them to explore and wonder what each one wants. What is most important in the relationship? What do you like? What do you not like?

For good lovers

Thus, in sexual matters, that breathless phrase "life is not measured by the times you breathe but by the moments when you are out of breath," is very applicable. The search for enjoyment, affection or orgasm can go through periods of dissatisfaction, blockage or trauma, that if you only look for explanations on the outside, in the body, you do not achieve any sense or a pleasant response to express love, which is the fundamental thing in the relationship.

Of course, there is negative mental programming, especially the one imposed subliminally by machismo, which presupposes that "women only enjoy sexuality psychologically." The truth is that orgasm is part of a process that women learn, while the male climax is more automatic and early. And hence it turns out that there are women who fake orgasms to not detune in a duo or because reaching the climax is not so important.

But how can we ensure that the expectations of having a sweet, deep relationship, with greater contemplation, contact, and caress are fulfilled in the couple we want? Perhaps, changing, not of the partner, but convictions, reprogramming what mentally produces negative responses in the way relationships are established.

In this way, there are traces of a map to apply neurolinguistic programming in the life of a couple. Consuelo Martínez gives sexuality a greater dimension, which is not restricted only to genitality, but also highlights the importance that mental structures have on affectivity, desires, and relationships.

The good lovers, in short, are those who know that the map is not the territory. But they do know how to get to the "You are here" point.

The most Powerful Mind-Power Tool

1- Self Test emotional: We should often ask ourselves how we are, and if we perceive that there is a lingering emotion, or attention, we should ask what is the message that brings. The answer does not usually take long if we are honest with ourselves.

Let's also learn to name emotions. Let's ask ourselves in what way it did not sit well if we feel that someone else's comment did not sit well with us. Has it caused anger? Frustration? Sadness? Envy? If we manage to give a name to the emotions, it will be easier to recognize and speak to them over time.

2- Let us live the Present with voluntary intensity: We do not invest too much energy in the memories of the past and the expectations of the future. The past does not exist now. It is the memory of present moments that have passed. The future does not exist now. It is the projection of future moments that may come at some point. Sant Agustí already wrote it sixteen hundred years ago. In essence, consciousness is diluted if we overthink about the past and future, and it does not allow us to maintain contact with the Present, with reality.

3- Let's do different things: If we always get up at 7, let's get up one day at 6.30 and another day at 7.05. If we still drink apple and orange juice, let us add a mango and a papaya juice to our palates. Let's learn to do everyday things with the hand that we use the least, let's play with our bodies and with the things that surround us to stimulate adaptation to something new, although small. A brain that adapts quickly is a brain that does not stagnate in the problem, but naturally seeks other (emotional) opportunities and outlets.

4- Let us grant ourselves the power to choose what kind of thoughts to have: In the same way as when we go to the market to buy things. We have more or less definite ideas of what we are going to buy when we are aware of a constant negative thought, let's ask ourselves: Is this thought useful for my personal development? Does it help me to be a better person? Can it help me achieve a loving and content mood? Is it essential for the development of my skills at work or in relationships with others?

If the answer is no, then we thank the thought and "we accompany him to the exit." Emotions and feelings should never be cast or denied or mistreated. We always accept its existence, and we intervene when choosing what stays and what does not.

5- Let's learn to smile more. At first, it may seem forced and uncomfortable, but over time a genuine and harmonious smile will emerge. Let's start in the morning in the mirror: we smile at each other and pay ourselves a compliment like "Today you are doing super well, flat!

You deserve it !!" Let's be ironic; let's say nonsense from time to time; let's be able to take ourselves not so seriously. Life is short and is to love.

6- Let's be grateful. Let us thank everyone and everything. The world smiles at those who smile. The world gives to whom it provides. If you think you could spend so much, well, you're wrong. Thanksgiving is an act of love and trust. It never is enough. If it seems too much, it is because you are afraid of love.

CHAPTER 2

WHAT'S EMOTIONAL MANIPULATION?

You may already be used to hearing about emotional manipulation, the manipulator's behavior, and the victims he leaves in his path. Undoubtedly, it is one of the behaviors that generate the most harmful effects on the victim, mainly due to its silent and lethal character.

The emotional manipulator has a perfectly defined action plan in his head. He knows his victim's weaknesses and how to remove his defenses to impose himself. He acts as if he were the victim, and the other is to blame: he convinces the other person to give him a reason and do what he wants.

They manage to generate certain emotions in the other, depending on what interests them. The plan, as we said earlier, is already outlined. They do not hesitate and use all possible means to manipulate the other's will, using it as a tool for their purposes.

Cognitive dissonance: the origin of emotional manipulation

Manipulators use what in psychology is called "cognitive dissonance." The cognitive dissonance refers to the internal conflict that we feel when we have two contradictory or incompatible ideas in our minds, or when a thought does not fit into our belief system or behavior.

This internal conflict, this tension that corrodes the thought, ends up generating a very curious result. We deceive ourselves to avoid this sensation of cognitive uprooting where we enter without realizing it. This sense of internal inconsistency stuns us to such an extent that we will do our best to eliminate it.

We need to feel an internal coherence between what we feel and what we think, between our beliefs and our attitudes... between what we think and how we act. When we find ourselves at this crossroads, we will leave it at any cost, even if caught in the hands of self-deception.

Self-deception is the subterfuge par excellence of all cognitive dissonance

We will do everything necessary not to endure this feeling of internal inconsistency for long. We will avoid becoming aware of all information that increases this dissonance and "closes our eyes" to anything that may destabilize us even more.

The emotional manipulator knows how to act in the face of cognitive dissonance by deceiving himself to achieve his goal. For example, some people are unable to end some relationships; then, they will do everything to reverse the situation and for the other to end this relationship.

Jorge wants to leave Maria because he met another girl for whom he felt a special "connection." Maria, on the other hand, doesn't know any of this, doesn't want to end the courtship because she is very much in love with him.

Faced with this situation, Jorge will do everything possible for Maria to end this relationship once and for all. Later, she will feel the sole responsibility for the end. Jorge will say: "Oh, no! You were the one who left me, and I never said that!"

The handler transfers the blame to the other and gets rid of it

He is faced with the discomfort caused by the confrontation between who he is and what he would like to be, someone loyal. What is being done at that moment is that Jorge chooses to manipulate Maria emotionally so that she can resolve the situation... be the culprit for the breakup. Maria probably does not understand what is happening, because few can conceive having a partner who does this. On the other hand, Jorge's behavior may not be conscious.

In this case, Jorge does not see himself ending a relationship, much less than the reason is that another girl appeared in his life. In his mind, he doesn't want the role of the villain in the relationship, and to protect himself, and he plays the victim. In order not to accept this reality, not to assume his responsibility, he manipulates Maria until the rope breaks definitively, regardless of how much she may suffer.

If Maria is the person who left him, he will need not feel guilty about wanting to leave her for someone else. Because it "goes bad" and can tarnish your reputation. Instead, in this way, he resolves the internal conflict and "benefits" from this battle.

For all these reasons, emotional manipulation is often the result of cognitive chaos from which the person seeks to get rid of it anyway. They will look for an executor, a culprit who will make them victims or put them in a situation that justifies their thoughts or behavior.

The other will always be to blame. They will always be the unhappy victims in their relationships overtaken by emotional manipulation.

Types of Emotional Manipulation

The very word manipulation already calls for something unpleasant and undesirable. One of the types of manipulation is emotional manipulation, and often a person consciously allows it to happen because he does not know how to deal with it. This section will explain some of the actions of emotional manipulators and how to deal with them.

Cheating the victim: Is something we face every day. They never want to take responsibility for their actions, but constantly play the victim and blame others for something they have done wrong. As a result, someone apologizes to them in the end, because they are skilled in playing the role of someone helpless.

Presenting their problem as bigger: Is also a common occurrence. If a person starts complaining about their problem, they will immediately start comparing. Even if your two problems are not connected, they will find a way to connect them and thus tell us to "tie-up," because no one has a bigger problem than them.

"Gaslighting": Has the consequence that the person who is a victim of gaslighting begins to wonder if he is sane because the emotional manipulator begins to convince him that he has heard or seen something wrong. In that way, they establish control because people often react to it by starting to question themselves, and it mostly ends by convincing themselves to imagine.

Making jokes: Is sometimes very difficult to recognize as manipulation because people generally do not associate humor with anything bad. However, there is a difference between a harmless joke and harassment. Emotional manipulators will constantly belittle us and deliberately provoke us where they know it hurts, claiming that they are just kidding, to establish superiority over someone. If someone decides to oppose them, he will immediately blame them for being too sensitive or accusing them of making a scene, maybe even in front of friends and acquaintances. This allows them to behave as they wish because no one likes to be labeled as a "party breaker".

The question is, how to protect yourself from emotional manipulators? The most important thing of all is to learn to recognize when someone is trying to manipulate us. Once we do that, the next step is not to let them have control over us. Ask yourself, why allow yourself to feel unnecessarily bad? It's easier said than done because they often play on our empathy, and it's hard for some people to stop it. However, the sooner we start trying, the easier it will be later. Although sometimes it seems to us that there is no way out of the black hole, we are the ones who set the boundaries, and if we allow the manipulators to cross them once, they will do it again.

Hold on to yourself, and don't let others sway you.

Behavioral and Character Traits of Manipulators

Throughout your life, you will encounter manipulative people, who pursue their selfish purposes, for which they have no qualms about causing harm to you.

Generally, manipulative people have no qualms or compassion when they find a new victim for their plans since they are individuals dedicated to exploiting other people's weaknesses to achieve their benefit, regardless of what they have to do for it.

The manipulative method used in this approach focuses on emotional blackmail, involving people with false words and deeds. In this way, their victims trust and yield to the supposed good intention of this manipulative mind, which pretends to feel sympathy and appreciation for others.

Hence the danger posed by manipulative people to anyone's life, as for them, there is no moral limit or obstacle between their goal and themselves. This allows them to easily crush, use, and dispose of people affected by the way they act.

Despite knowing the threat that manipulative people pose in their life, it is quite difficult to differentiate them into a group of acquaintances or coworkers since you can even fall victim to someone without realizing it until you are affected by their bad influence.

That is why we present five typical characteristics of a manipulator, to help you identify and recognize this type of predator that lurks in your social circles.

Five common traits in manipulative people

Innate speakers

Manipulative people demand their best speech skills to convince their victims of their false good intentions to deal with the gift of speech effectively.

They can transform any situation they find themselves in to convince others of their innocence. Coming to create a false image in the minds of those who fall for their mind games.

They maintain excessive control over the situation, always obtaining the greatest benefit in exchange for others' hard work. His word tends to confuse and manipulate his victims efficiently, to the point of remaining unaware of a bad way of acting.

Manipulative people are greedy

Manipulators do not pursue a simple goal that they can achieve on their own; on the contrary, they are always looking for a greater objective that constantly compresses their victims.

The hunger for power and control is also a reflection of the great ego that manipulative people tend to possess—those who over-rely on their manipulation to the point of feeling invincible, lest they set future limits.

They tend to assume the role of the victim

Being a victim implies great vulnerability and innocence, so it is the preferential role of manipulative people. Since people around them never think that the victim is the victim.

In this way, they manipulate other people emotionally, playing with their feelings. Therefore, confrontation with a manipulator can make you believe that he is the victim, and you are the aggressor.

Create a false image of the need

Piety is the emotion that manipulative people tend to hold on to. To do this, they use an image of weakness and fragility, to which their victims fall easily, wanting to help someone in need.

After deceiving people with their false need, a manipulator makes his victims feel responsible for their health, food, money, and any other benefits they can obtain from that individual.

Manipulative people always lie

Inevitably, lying is part of any manipulator's repertoire. They deal with this ability naturally, without showing doubts or any characteristic that allows their victims to detect the truth behind their false facade.

Manipulative people are masters of lies, to the point of lying in any aspect of their lives, regardless of whether it is minimal or important. Because, through deception, they can approach the goal they are pursuing.

For lack of a moral compass, there is no limit to the lies of a manipulator. For him, lies are part of the tools he needs to achieve his goal, regardless of who he causes harm.

CHAPTER 3
PSYCHOLOGICAL MANIPULATION TECHNIQUES

The sophisticated technique that many fraudsters use to gain benefits is to manipulate people. Human psychology is so powerful that it can be controlled. In the commercial talks process, the sides seek to place pressure on each other to support their position. And to defend yourself from outside threats, you need to learn to know various forms of coercion.

It's usually hidden away. It's harder to suppress the will openly. It needs a person who is easily exposed to it. There are very few of them and the hidden coercion of individuals is being used in this respect.

The multiple arts of management

Psychology is multiple sciences. And the art of manipulation is direct proof of that. There are a huge number of methods you can use to learn to control a person. But no manipulator would use all means. They usually choose some of the most appropriate methods. Why is human manipulation so popular?

With the help of management skills, you can not only influence the actions of the interlocutor but also achieve your goals.

You have to feel the mood of the people

It would help if you did not think that everyone is subject to management. Some people are difficult to hypnotize. Therefore, they are also not subject to manipulation. The attackers are trying to avoid such people. How do you know who to avoid and who can be controlled? Manipulations by people, psychology - to be a professional in these areas, you need to feel the interlocutor's mood. Otherwise, all abilities will be reduced to zero.

1. Distribution of Attention

We, therefore, remind you of the still current Techniques of manipulation.

A key element of social control is a strategy of distraction or obstruction that will distract the public from important issues and changes that the political and economic elite decide through continuous interference by placing insignificant information. Distraction strategy is important for preventing public interest in basic knowledge from science, economics, psychology, neurobiology, and cybernetics.

2. Create Problems and Offer A Solution

The method is also called "problem-reaction-solution." This method creates a problem, a "situation" that provokes reactions in public, after which solutions are offered that would, under normal circumstances, be opposed by the public.

For example: Let urban violence develop and intensify or arrange bloody attacks so that the public can demand new security laws and rules on its own, albeit to the detriment of personal freedom. Or: create an economic crisis and accept the recession as a necessary evil and ultimately reduce social rights and reduce public services.

3. Strategy of Graduality Of Change

Make the public accept the unacceptable, i.e., apply gradual acceptance of change, drop by drop, step by step.

4. Use of Children's Language

A better future facilitates their acceptance.

5. Disposal Strategy

Another way to prepare the public for unpopular changes is to announce them much earlier, in advance. They should also be presented as "painful and necessary" to gain public consent for future changes. People do not feel all the weight of change at once, because they get used to the very idea of change. Also, the common hope for most advertisements aimed at the general public use speech, arguments, characters, and especially children's intonations, as if addressing small children or mentally underdeveloped people. The more they want to mislead the viewers, the more they apply infantile tones. When addressing adults as if you were addressing children, we achieve two beneficial effects: the public suppresses their critical awareness, and the message has a stronger effect on people.

6. Use of Emotions

Emotional abuse is a classic technique used to cause a short circuit in the process of reasonable judgment. Critical consciousness is replaced by emotional impulses (anger, fear, etc.).

7. Keep the Public in Ignorance And Average

Render the population incapable of recognizing the technology and techniques used to regulate and enslave it. The quality of education in the lower social strata should be as low or below average as possible so that the chasm between the upper and lower strata remains insurmountable.

8. Encouraging the Public to Be Satisfied with Its Average

The promotion of the public's attitude is that it is modern and desirable to be stupid, vulgar, and uneducated.

9. Creating A Feeling of Guilt

To lead a person to assume that he is the only one to blame for his failures, because of the weakness of his intellect, negligence, or lack of effort. Thus, instead of rebelling against the economic environment, the person does not act because he blames himself for mistakes, contributing to distressing societies whose sole function is to discourage intervention.

10. Getting to Know an Individual Better Than He Knows Himself

The rapid development of science in the last 50 years has

created a larger gap between the knowledge possessed by the average man and the knowledge possessed and used by the ruling elites.

The system can understand the common man better than he knows himself. This means that, in most cases, the system has more control and has more power over the individual than the individual has over himself.

CHAPTER 4

THE ROLE OF DEFENCE

Signs that You're Being Manipulated

There is a category of manipulators who try to influence people, fully aware of what they are doing. To manipulate is to persuade a person to fulfill one's will to gain profit. A person unconsciously manipulates from an early age. Already, preschoolers can use primitive manipulation techniques to get what they want from their parents.

Most adults also use manipulation techniques, but more often, they do it unknowingly. But there is a category of manipulators who try to influence people, fully aware of what they are doing. Such people are called energy vampires and maintaining close contact with them is sometimes very dangerous.

How to recognize who is in front of you—an experienced manipulator, aware of his actions, or just a person acting out of habit, unconsciously? Consider the following signs that you are being manipulated consciously.

1. The model of behavior

If we talk about experienced manipulators who are used to achieving their goals by controlling people through their subconscious fears and weaknesses, they differ in a certain behavior model. Conscious manipulations gradually lead to personality deformation. Several behavioral features are considered typical. The first thing you need to pay attention to is excessive, ostentatious emotionality.

Second, such people are attentive and observant, and you can notice how they sometimes peer at people. A professional manipulator will never listen to a person inattentively. He listens sympathetically, actively participates in conversations, can assent. And of course, the third—the manipulators take small pauses between the emotional reactions and the events that provoked them. This happens only because their body needs a little more time to synthesize emotions, which are often an instrument of control and influence.

2. Unpredictability

As a rule, it is impossible to predict such a person's words and actions in advance. This distinguishes manipulators—they have flexibility, and they always adjust their actions depending on the situation, and on how open the interlocutor is. Unpredictability is inherent in every person, but usually, the actions and words of such people in most cases can be predicted. Manipulators often use it as a technique that discourages the interlocutor, disorients, and plunges into confusion. It is at such moments that people are most open to manipulation, and one who uses this method of influence consciously often uses unpredictability.

3. The lack of direct answers

As a rule, an unconsciously manipulating person does not

care that their victim can figure it out. However, professionals know what they are doing and why, and are as cautious as possible in their speeches. Therefore, they often answer evasively or may even evade answers if it is not convenient for them to answer questions.

4. Inconsistency of gestures and emotions

This is a typical sign of insincerity that accompanies all the speech of manipulators using unclean tricks in dealing with people. You can replace the difference between what kind of emotional tone a person speaks and what his gestures are. As a rule, manipulators actively gesticulate, and it is difficult not to notice it. Unconscious manipulation is distinguished by the fact that a person does everything automatically, and the pros perfectly understand their insincerity and try to hide behind an emotional background.

5. Conversations in private

Each of us sometimes needs to discuss something with someone in private. This is the norm and does not contain any toxic elements. But a consciously manipulating person almost always calls his potential victim into a solitary conversation, since in this case, he will have to face the least resistance. A person who realizes that he plans to persuade someone through psychological pressure to fulfill his will not do this in public, where there is a high risk of exposure.

6. Valuation judgment

Pro manipulators use value judgment more often than

ordinary people. They intend to expose the world, people, phenomena, and actions in black or white, without shades. They have only "very good"—this is usually what is beneficial to them. And "very bad" is what they do not need at all.

7. Eye-to-eye look

As a rule, psychologists recommend recognizing liars and manipulators by a wandering gaze. People often look away when they are not completely sincere, but this is most often done by those who do this unconsciously. An energy vampire who knows his job, on the contrary, tries to look directly into the eyes of his interlocutor, and rarely looks away. Because of this gaze, people get confused quicker and can make concessions easier.

8. Speed

The manipulator, acting consciously, does not give the interlocutor time for thought and does it very skillfully. He requires an immediate response, and always adjusts the circumstances in such a way as to increase the likelihood of agreement. They do everything very quickly, do not insert pauses in conversations, and are always in a hurry. Modern psychologists have begun to study the fraud's problem to uncover as many criminal schemes as possible aimed at taking away other people's money. Relatively recently, psychologists around the world have become interested in the so-called "toxic charges." We are talking about fraudulent fundraising, allegedly for sick children. Law enforcement authorities have uncovered several such cases. And psychologists noted that in all messages of scammers, there was an emphasis on urgency.

9. The tendency to downplay

This is another psychological technique that is not always used consciously. The tendency to downplay is inherent in absolutely all categories of manipulating personalities, but those who do this consciously use this technique more often and more persistently. Such a person likes to periodically accept the victim's image because having caused pity in the interlocutor makes it easier for him to manage him.

10. Aura of hopelessness

If the manipulator acts consciously, it does not just play down, which thickens colors to hopelessness. The complete hopelessness that he can draw in the imagination of the interlocutor is not a reliable reflection of reality. The manipulator presents only negative facts, skillfully hiding the positive aspects and keeping silent about them.

To learn to recognize manipulators and understand whether they manipulate consciously or unconsciously, experience and practice are needed. Unfortunately, it is far from always possible to figure out an energy vampire right away, but with experience, this skill will come.

Factors that Make You Vulnerable to Manipulation

Manipulation comes into play in many of our relationships, but to what extent does it affect you? You are not exempt from others' influence; if you usually do things that you do not want at the suggestion of others, you may be a somewhat manipulatable person.

You need to understand that being a manipulatable person is something that many people around you can take advantage of. Being aware of this issue can make you reflect on how the opinion of others determines your behavior, to try to modify this aspect.

If you want to know to what extent other people take advantage of you and end up manipulating you, you should check for yourself if you are a manipulatable person. Through this simple test, we show you.

Test to know if you are a manipulatable person

- It makes me nervous when I realize that they are trying to blackmail me. T or F
- I consider that the opinion of others is something that matters a lot to me, sometimes even too much. T or F
- I usually have a hard time expressing my opinion and offering my point of view. T or F
- I generally do things to please others. T or F
- I need the approval of everyone, or most people. T or F
- When I make a mistake, I feel guilty and give many justifications. T or F
- If someone gets mad at me for not doing what he asks me, I do what is necessary so that he doesn't get angry. T or F

- I always try to follow social fads or trends. T or F
- I feel that my decisions are based primarily on the needs and wants of others. T or F
- I have a great need for other people to be okay with me. T or F
- If I realize that someone does not like my clothes, I will not wear them again. T or F
- I usually feel guilty about any anger from others. T or F

Answers:

Score one point for each true answer. If you have earned six or more points, you are a person who can become easy to manipulate by others.

You must be aware of this matter so that some people do not take advantage of you. Reflect on how you relate to your environment since you are in time to change this situation.

If you have scored less than 6 points, congratulations! You do not allow yourself to be influenced too much by others, value your opinions, and have your criteria to face life.

You don't need too much of the approval of others, and you know how to distinguish between what is your responsibility and what is not.

How to Defend Yourself from a Manipulative Person

Manipulation is a rather unpleasant word. Especially when it is used about your person. But, one way or another, each of us is faced with manipulation daily.

This can include both attempts by someone from the environment to influence our actions and decisions, as well as the usual impact on us of advertising from billboards or gadget displays.

Logically, you will immediately want to defend yourself against attempts by anyone to incline you to certain actions and deeds. Then it is necessary to understand what methods of protection against manipulation generally exist clearly. We'll talk about this.

How to resist manipulation in real life?

It is not difficult to protect oneself from manipulation. After all, everything has a recipe and solution. But before we touch on the topic of the mechanism of protection against manipulation, it is worth learning three basic and quite important points. Their understanding will help in using those techniques that will be described in the future.

So, three conditions must be observed:

Your speech and language should be clear and concise.

Your intonation should be appropriate to the situation and be intelligible.

Each of your answers to the replica of the manipulator (a person trying to impose his will and his decisions on you) must be thorough and confident.

Have you learned? Fine, then move on. After all, these

three aspects are based on everything that will be listed below. And below are the main ways to protect against manipulation, which were once painstakingly collected by the famous American social psychologist, Philip Zimbardo.

Methods of protection against manipulation

Do you feel that a colleague, relative or any other person is trying to impose their opinion on you, forcing you to do what they need?

Such actions can be either in the form of an active emotional conviction of the interlocutor or in an attempt to "put pressure on pity," or even blame something. To become the master of our own decisions, we will look at 12 ways that will certainly help to resist manipulations of this nature.

Recognize and mirror manipulation

"Exit the template."

This is a method that consists of the following - learn to behave in a dialogue, going out of your typical form, and manner of communication. Try on yourself the role of a person with the opposite character. For example, react as the manipulator does not expect at all. The main thing—do not even think while making excuses or bickering.

Accept your mistakes and shortcomings.

State clearly that you made a mistake. Having agreed on what you are accused of, you will disarm your interlocutor and discard the burden of unnecessary obligations based on remorse.

Do not be fooled by the manipulator imposing his picture of the world.

Suggest an alternative to how you see the situation under discussion. Be prepared to take a step back in time and declare your rejection of the vision that is being imposed on you by another person.

Do not be afraid of a short-term refusal of goods.

Which may follow the termination of contracts with the manipulator (the same money or other material resources). If a person openly imposes on you actions that are beneficial to him, break your relationship, and consider the knowledge gained from this as a useful experience.

Be prepared to refuse to communicate with the manipulator.

This item is paired with the previous one but is still somewhat different. This is about intangible things. Do not be afraid to say the word "enough" to the person manipulating you. Accept that you are self-sufficient and able to live without being favored by anyone. It can be both a refusal from companionship and the sympathy of the opposite sex.

Do not let them rush you.

Often the manipulator rushes you in making decisions. And he can do it skillfully and quite emotionally. Do not fall for such tricks, in any situation, take time to think.

Insist on clear and concise explanations of a given situation.

Also, do not respond to provocations aimed at making you stupid. If any explanation was ambiguous—require specifics!

Don't play too much in the host-guest relationship model.

Being in conditions that ascribe guest behavior to you, do not get too carried away with this role. Indeed, often such rules significantly limit your freedom of action, hiding behind the generally accepted model of behavior.

Do not expect from a person baseless sympathy and even love.

This is one of the most important principles on which defense mechanisms against manipulation are based. No, that doesn't mean that you need to expect a trick and set it up everywhere. It only means that it's worth looking at relationships (especially with strangers) a little more pragmatically.

Try yourself as an impartial and cold person.

Oddly enough, at the same time, you can safely remain a kind, sympathetic, and a good person. However, critical thinking and evaluating other people's actions without an emotional component will significantly increase your chances of a calm and confident achievement of your own goals.

Eradicate guilt dictated to you by someone from the outside.

Consider mistakes as experience and try not to make them, but never "digest" everything that has already passed in your head. It is the regular experience of situations from the past, based on a sense of guilt that can unsettle and make you subject to a human manipulator.

Act not based on established habits and laws, but the basis of your judgments.

Accept the idea that you can change—you are a living person. Even if you're used to expecting one thing, but you decide to do otherwise, you have every right to do so.

Doing as profitable does not mean to be bad.

Do not forget that almost everyone in the world is trying to capitalize on it. Often, people differ only in the fact that some accept this idea, while others consider it something completely unacceptable and themselves suffer because of this. If you want to succeed, consider yourself the first type. This does not mean that you will become selfish. On the contrary, you can look at many things with a cold head and free yourself from the shackles of far-fetched obligations and rules that manipulators skillfully use for their purposes.

Practical Tips for Dealing with Predators

When dealing with an emotional predator, we should have a good social and psychological support.

The victim of an emotional predator does not always have adequate resources to cope with this behavior. Thus, it is common that it is completely conditioned to the personality of the first, who feels the victim of a psychological prison and trapped in turn by fear.

In these cases, in addition to making use of adequate psycho-emotional skills, it is always vital that we have social and healthcare support. As striking as it may seem to us, all of us can fall into such damaging links at some point in time. Regardless of our gender, social position, or previous experience.

The emotional predator inhabits almost any setting. Furthermore, there is a narcissistic profile sometimes behind these behaviors, a personality type that highly specialized in psychological manipulation, blackmail, and domination. Knowing how to act is key in all cases.

Identify the emotional predator

There is a first aspect that we must take into account. We must be sensitive and know how to react in time to all processes of emotional predation. We cannot forget that this reality occurs too frequently and defines a highly common type of psychological abuse.

To do this, we must put aside the blame and gradually abandon the position of tolerance, recognizing that the person we are with may have a possible personality disorder or simply be someone with dangerous behavior.

Therefore, it is important to understand their tactics and how they work, counting as far as possible with psychological help and support from our environment.

Let's see some characteristics.

How is the emotional predator?

- He yearns for control at all times.
- He despises and humiliates the other person. In case he offers reinforcements or positive acts; it will be done for personal interest or to get something.
- He manipulates reality, makes us believe that we are wrong or that we are naive.
- He victimizes himself to be in control.
- Ironic, critical, sarcastic language.
- Grandiose airs.
- He punishes us often with indifference and with the idea of severing the relationship.
- Projects the blame on us.

As a curiosity, according to a study carried out at the University of Innsbruck, Germany, by doctors Ursa Nagler and Katharina J. Reiter, the emotional predator is highly skilled in Emotional Intelligence. However, be careful because that ability is used to control others.

Stop justifying yourself

It is important to keep this message in mind when you are faced with an emotional predator. The victim will indeed want to justify himself since the aggressor's speech is riddled with lies, but the explanations and justifications will only lead to getting more stuck at that moment:

- The emotional predator will use all the mistakes and inaccuracies that his victim has made against them, even if they had good intentions.
- Therefore, silence is better, since anything we do or say can turn against us.
- If we are facing a moment of separation, the harassment process can be carried out by phone or through messages.

For such cases, it is recommended, if possible, to change the number or email, filter them, or have a third person to help us. It is whoever intervenes since if it is the victim who responds again, they can re-immerse themselves in the process of emotional predation, destabilizing their separation and independence.

Act

As the mental process of separation progresses, and the victim finds himself strong and resilient, he can change his strategy and act firmly, without fear.

The crisis will allow the victim's life to be reborn again. We must end this link clearly and definitively.

To resist

It is important to know that to resist psychologically, you have to have some kind of support that is capable of restoring the victim's self-confidence that has been lost.

Valid supports are content to be by the victim's side, available when the victim needs them, without making judgments or being fooled by reproaches and manipulations.

Further, it is advisable to go to professionals (psychologists, psychiatrists, etc.) to help us reestablish our well-being and personal autonomy, as well as to recover our confidence and face our fears.

Justice intervention

It may happen that a crisis or a conflict of this type can only be resolved with justice. However, in these processes, the provision of evidence is necessary. This is where there are usually more complications because humiliations, contempt, insults, and offenses are difficult to demonstrate unless there is a third party when they occur, which may be the key.

It is also suggested to keep all written documents that can be recognized as evidence. It is an arduous process, and full of uncertainty, since many judges are suspicious.

Perhaps the only way to protect the victim is to establish rigid judicial orders and avoid any contact between the parties. Being finally, a matter of justice, the adoption of adequate protection measures to avoid the resurgence of the relationship of emotional predation.

CHAPTER 5

THE ART OF BODY LANGUAGE

Why is body language an art? Why is it so crucial to understanding getting better at decoding the opposite sex? One simple answer may answer these questions: most communication is considered non-verbal, up to 90%. Those who use non-verbal communication of 90% are very good at it and have practiced it more than once. Think about it this way: can you use non-verbal communication to tell a person how you feel, and what you think? Probably not.

Thus, you fall into the 70-80% of people who lack sufficient non-verbal competencies. Those who fall in the 20-30% of people who are capable of non-verbal communication, find themselves lucky because it is a powerful skill. What are the keys to success, then? All circumstances are unique, but patterns are permanent, so the following things to be looked for are not set in stone but are a great guide to construct from.

The first and largest type of nonverbal contact is with your eyes. One cannot overemphasize how important the initial eye-contact is because this is the first form of non-verbal contact that one normally encounters when communicating with an opposite-sex person. This doesn't mean that if somebody stares at you, they're interested in you and you should look back. NO! NO! It is all focused on contextual situations. This is an appropriate assumption in a bar because it befits the atmosphere. But, if you're enjoying a family dinner at the restaurant, you're likely to have something on your chin or mouth. So, there are certain ways to tell if someone, in this case, is also trying to communicate with you non-verbally.

The transition from eye language to body language is much faster in the first situation at the bar; therefore, it is easier to decipher as a purposeful nonverbal communication. In the restaurant's second scenario, eye language is the prominent form of non-verbal communication, since the person cannot use their body to communicate their feelings/thought. Therefore, if there are repeated occasions where eye contact continues for longer than 1.7 seconds, this can be viewed as purposeful flirting. Why those 1.7s? Based on many studies conducted by people who are interested in interactions with others, most of the situations that include eye flirting last for about 1.5-1.7s per eye contact. Also, if you want to test whether they look back at you or not because you started to look at them, using your peripheral vision is simple. Try and catch them looking at you. If this occurs on more than one occasion, then your initial thoughts are confirmed. Rule of thumb, if the eye language studies concentrate on the language of the brain, DO NOT start incorporating subtle facial gestures because you may look stupid and give the wrong impression if done wrong.

The Five C's of Body Language

Do you want to know exactly what people think when they talk to you? Their lips say yes, but they say no with their eyes and their bodies. We unconsciously pick up on those signals. Have you ever had a bad feeling about someone who's been justified?

The human ability to understand body language meaning was essential to life. The earliest cavemen wanted to know whether others were friends or a threat, so they easily determined this by reading their non-verbal signals. One Princeton study found a first impression took 100 milliseconds to form.

Body language goes beyond detecting threats. Protecting ourselves is about human nature. Sometimes that means masking our real feelings and intentions. Decoding such motives lets you know whether you are interested in a future date, a working relationship is going poorly, or someone is trying to take advantage of you. This won't hurt, either, as a party trick.

We can understand body language. If you've ever "seen" someone wasn't interested in you, you've picked up the language of their body. You can appear to read minds by learning more about the more than 30,000 unconscious clues we send off.

Body language goes in both directions. You will learn to interpret another person's actions, while others can read your thoughts and intentions. Be mindful of this so that you can align your body language with your intentions, including emphasizing authenticity and not signs of deceit.

Charles Darwin believed that six facial expressions were genetically inherited: joy, sorrow, anxiety, disgust, surprise, and rage. Later work verified that such terms are used and accepted in the world.

Perhaps you'd like to brush up on how to understand body language. It's not enough to memorize body movements and expressions to know what someone feels; a movement is often not a true signal, but a spontaneous gesture. To further refine your body language skills, you will need to apply the following 5 C's to what you are doing.

1. Context

Our eyes are moving in different directions, depending on what part of our brain we control. We search for constructed images (up and right for visual, right for auditory and down and right for kinesthetic) and left for recollected images (and again, up / left for visual, left for auditory, down / left for kinesthetic).

To check that, ask a friend a question like, "What is your favorite song's second line?" (They would look to the left) or "What if I were a woman/man?" (They would look up and down). They usually look left when they remember something, while their eyes flit to the right for imagination.

Does that mean that someone lies when they look right? It depends on a lot of things; meaning is one of those.

Looking left into a courtroom may be a sign of deceit. But what if the jury is on the left and the accused gazes at their reaction nervously? Are they always looking left, or was it only in response to a particular question? You can already see how a manufacturing environment can make someone look more guilty than their natural self would produce.

Say you're talking to someone, avoiding eye contact, looking at your phone, and folding your arms. They assume you are bored but knowing "Signal A = B" is not enough. We are not living in a vacuum, and our world constantly affects us. Think about what's going on in the nonverbal signal before you leap to a conclusion.

Firstly, what's the chat about? Has the other person suddenly shifted his or her body language when a particular topic arose? It could be the subject that renders them uncomfortable. Try to change the subject then see what's going on.

Second, consider your surroundings. Crossed arms are a sign of defensiveness, which creates a barrier, but it may be cold and they're just trying to keep warm. Look for all the details. Perhaps their ex just walked in or they have bad memories of that place.

Finally, think about the person you meet. They may be checking their phone because they're expecting some important news, they've received a message that's putting them on edge, or they've had a stressful day and have not yet disconnected.

Contextual awareness will save you from embarrassment. Imagine conversing with an attractive man or woman. You think they flirt from the way they turn their body towards you. Often a woman's interested in you when she crosses her legs toward you. Other signs of interest are leaning in and shifting their body to face you.

To get meaning from the body language, look at the context. During a date, aspects of the person's body towards you are strong signs of attraction, but there are other circumstances where people can expose their attitude to you; therapists, interviewees, and sales staff know how to do that.

Never underestimate contextual meaning. The way someone conducts themselves at work, with their mates, and on a date is very different. The atmosphere and the attitude of an individual has a profound impact on how they behave. Don't apply the same rules for every situation.

2. Clusters

People send off hundreds of signs in body language. It's easy to hone in on one thing after learning a body language text, e.g., the way they rub their nose (which can indicate lying) or their upper arm (which can indicate attraction). By doing so, you miss the other signs people are sending off.

There is nothing in solitary confinement. While talking about sports or baseball, the word "bat" takes on a different meaning. If a friend rubs her eyes, you can agree that she's bored. Look at the picture as a whole, and you might also note that she is yawning and rubbing her temples; she's just really tired.

If she is rubbing her eyes, avoiding contact with your eyes, crossing her arms defensively and pouting, you can put the pieces together and know that she's upset. You will strengthen your friendship by reading your friend's feelings. You might inquire whether she is okay, or whether she needs a cup of coffee.

Search for three to five behavioral elements that go together before making an assumption. Eye contact, laughing, gently rubbing your shoulder, playing with her hair, and even revealing her wrists (showing vulnerability) is a typical sign of female flirting. It's not enough to see just one of those signs to deduce that she is flirting with you.

Note how much a behavioral cluster deviates from the normal behavior of that person. Your colleague may stumble over their words, move their eyes around quickly, hunch their shoulders, and speak quietly. They may be lying or afraid, but if they still act like this, the chances are that they're just a nervous person.

Ask yourself for every possible reason when you catch one piece of body language. Maybe that girl smiled at you because she's a smiley person, and she crossed her legs to point away from you because she feels more relaxed physically that way. Wait for several arrows before making your deductions to point toward the same thing.

3. Congruence

Imagine a man stopping you down the street and telling you the wonders of the commodity he sells. His words are meant to win you over, but a glance at his body language shows you he cannot be trusted. Do his words fit his actions?

These are congruent because words and acts tell the same story. When lying, people usually avoid eye contact, blink more than normal, and become anxious. When people say the truth, they gesture with palms up. The motion is a sign that they have nothing to conceal. Although body language reveals the facts, a story may sound convincing:

When somebody's words, tone of voice, and body language are in sync, you get a true signal. When your girlfriend says, "Honestly, I'm great!" you pick up an incongruent symbol as she crosses her arms and turns her body away from you.

Know how your body is betraying your true intentions of trying to match it to your thoughts. If you're trying to persuade a prospective boss to be comfortable in your job, make sure your body language suits your doing. I've found video creation is a good form of self-analysis to increase your body language awareness.

An open stance, leaning back a little and taking up plenty of room implies confidence while hunching your shoulders, forming a physical barrier (with arms, legs, or items), taking in as little space as possible implies the opposite.

4. Consideration

Consideration implies "using someone else's feet." Effective communication has to take into account the audience, i.e., the views of the audience, context, attitude, level of education, etc. Make an effort to think of the audience, their desires, feelings, and problems. Ensure the audience's self-respect is maintained, and their emotions are not harmed. Change your words in a message to suit the needs of the audience while completing your message. Considerable communication features shall be as follows:

Emphasize your approach to the "you."

Empathize with the audience and show public interest. That will encourage the public to react positively.

Give the viewers optimism. Emphasize "what's possible" instead of "what's impossible." Lay emphasis on such positive words as jovial, committed, thank you, warm, healthy, help, etc.

5. Culture

You come across a man who touches you while talking to you. Touching isn't completely inappropriate; he just brushes your arm lightly, catches you as he smiles, and sits close to you.

Physical contact is typically an attractive sign. A single touch's sense differs across cultures. People from New York or London need a great deal of personal space, while cultures from the Middle East or South America naturally touch as a sign of friendship. They may find your inability to make physical contact cold and unfriendly. When somebody's words, tone of voice, and body language are in sync, you get a real signal.

Understanding how the gestures vary from culture to culture is becoming increasingly important. Though nodding your head up and down usually means "yes," it means "no" for Eskimos and Belgians (whereas shaking your head from side to side means "yes").

Know the patterns of the body language of the cultures you come across. In Western culture, eye contact is a representation of interest, respect, and trust. Don't believe a lack of eye contact often indicates timidity or rudeness. Extended eye contact is seen as intrusive and awkward in a variety of Asian, African, or Latin American cultures.

Understand how cultures will disagree about a word's meaning. In America, the A-OK symbol (a circle with your thumb and index finger) is used to signify that all is OK. In the Middle East, Latin America, or Germany, this is a rude gesture. The reverse "heart" sign (holding two fingers away with the back of your hand) is as bad as giving anyone in the UK a "finger."

Reading body language is harder than memorizing a series of signals. Anything from a person's childhood and personality to their present mood and the setting they're in can influence what their body tells you. By looking at the larger image and using the 5 C's of body language, you will soon be able to tell others what is really in mind.

The Subconscious Mind and The Limbic Brain System

In this section, we will talk about the limbic system, the neocortex of their history of occurrence, and major functions.

Limbic system

The limbic system of the brain is a combination of complex neuroregulatory structures of the brain. This system is not limited to just a few functions—it performs a number of the most important tasks for a person. The purpose of the limbus is to regulate higher mental functions and special processes of higher nervous activities, from simple charm and alertness to cultural emotions, memories, and sleep.

History

The limbic system of the brain was formed long before the neocortex began to form. It is the oldest hormonal-instinctive structure of the brain responsible for the survival of the subject. For long evolution, it is possible to form 3 main goals of the survival system:

- Domination - A manifestation of superiority in various parameters
- Food - The nutrition of the subject
- Reproduction - The transfer of the genome to the next generation

Because man has animal roots, the limbic system is present in the human brain. Initially, a reasonable man had only an influence that affects the physiological state of the body. Over time, communication evolved according to the type of vocalization. Individuals who were able to convey their condition with the help of emotions survived. Over time, the emotional perception of reality took shape more and more. Such evolutionary stratification has allowed people to unite into groups, groups into tribes, tribes into migration, and others into entire nations. American researcher Paul Mac-Lin first discovered the limbic system in 1952.

System structure

Anatomically, the limbus includes areas of the paleocortex (ancient cortex), the archicortex (old cortex), part of the neocortex (new cortex), and some subcortex structures (caudate nucleus, amygdala, pale sphere). The listed names of different types of crust denote their formation at a particular time of evolution.

Many neuroscience experts have addressed the question of which structures belong to the limbic system. The latter includes many structures:

- Cingular gyrus.
- Hippocampus.
- Ribbon for ribbon.
- Parahippocampal gyrus.
- Zubati gyrus.
- Amygdala.
- Transparent partition cores.
- Mastoid bodies.
- The central gray matter of the water supply to the brain.

- Scented bulb, triangle, and fragrant tract.
- Anterior and middle nuclei of optic tubercle.
- Cord core.
- Midbrain nuclei.
- A collecting system of pathways that ensures communication between visceral brain structures.

The system is closely related to the reticular formation system (the structure responsible for brain activation and the state of wakefulness). The anatomy of the limbic complex rests on the gradual stratification of one part onto another. So above lies the cingulate gyrus, and further down:

- Corpus callosum.
- Vault.
- Mammary body.
- Tonsil.
- Hippocampus.

The peculiarity of the visceral brain is its rich connection with other structures, which consist of complex pathways and two-way connections. This system of branches forms a complex of closed circles, which creates the conditions for prolonged excitation circulation in the limbo.

Functional limbic system

The visceral brain actively receives and processes information from the outside world. What is the limbic system responsible for? The limbus is one of those structures that work in real-time, allowing the body to adapt effectively to environmental conditions.

The human limbic system in the brain performs the following function:

- Formation of emotions, feelings, and experiences. Through the prism of emotions, a person subjectively assesses objects and the phenomenon of the environment.
- Memory. This function is performed by the hippocampus, which is located in the structure of the limbic system. Mnestic processes are provided by echo processes—a circular motion of excitation in closed neural circuits of the seahorse.
- Selection and correction of appropriate behavior models.
- Learning, retraining, fear, and aggression.
- Development of spatial skills.
- Defensive and food search behavior.
- Express speech.
- Acquisition and maintenance of various phobias.
- Work on the odor system.
- Caution reaction, preparation for action.
- Regulation of sexual and social behavior. There is a concept of emotional intelligence—the ability to recognize the emotions of people around you.

When expressing emotions, a reaction occurs that manifests itself in changes in blood pressure, skin temperature, respiratory rate, pupil reactions, sweating, hormonal mechanisms, and much more.

Perhaps among women, the question arises as to how to include the limbic system in men. However, the answer is simple: there is no way. For all men, limbus works completely (except for patients). This is justified by evolutionary processes, when a woman in almost all periods of history has been engaged in raising a child, which involves a deep emotional impact, and thus a deep development of the emotional brain. Unfortunately, men no longer achieve a woman's limbo level.

The development of the limbic system in infants largely depends on the type of upbringing and the overall relationship to it. A stern look and a cold smile do not contribute to the development of the limbic complex, unlike hugs and sincere smiles.

Interaction with the neocortex

Numerous pathways tightly connect the neocortex and limbic system. Thanks to this unification, these two structures from one whole of the mental sphere of man: they unite the mental component with the emotional. The new bark acts as a regulator of animal instincts. Human thought, as a rule, undergoes a series of cultural and moral inspections before taking any spontaneous action caused by emotions. In addition to controlling emotions, the neocortex also has an ancillary effect. The feeling of hunger occurs in the depths of the limbic system, and already in the highest cortical centers that regulate behavior, they look for food.

Such a brain structure at the time did not bypass the

father of psychoanalysis, Sigmund Freud. The psychologist claimed that every neurosis is formed under the yoke of suppressing sexual and aggressive instincts. Of course, there was no data on limbo at the time of his work, but a great scientist speculated about similar devices in the brain. Thus, the more cultural and moral layers (superego - neocortex) in an individual, the more his primary animal instincts are suppressed (id - limbic system).

Violations and their consequences

Based on the fact that the limbic system is responsible for different functions, this set may be susceptible to different damages. Like other brain structures, the limbus can be exposed to injury and other harmful factors, including tumors with bleeding.

Syndromes of the destruction of the limbic system are rich in quantities, and the main ones are the following:

- **Dementia.** The development of diseases such as Alzheimer's and Pick's syndrome is associated with atrophy of the complex limbic system, especially in the localization of the hippocampus.
- **Epilepsy.** Organic hippocampal disorders lead to the development of epilepsy.
- **Pathological anxiety and phobias.** Disorder of amygdala activity leads to mediator imbalance, which, in turn, is accompanied by emotional disturbance, including anxiety. A phobia is an irrational fear of a harmless subject. Also, neurotransmitter imbalance causes depression and mania.

The most powerful techniques you can use to fake your body language and manipulate Anyone's

We all want people to trust us. Trust means that someone relies on you to do what you say you will do or to act like the person you say you are.

That's why it's especially crucial to earning the trust of those you work with. When people trust you, they are much more likely to believe in you, bond with you, and buy from you. Your actions ultimately determine whether you will earn someone's trust; however, your verbal communication and body language also play a big role.

Given that studies show that the vast majority of the messages we send are transmitted through our body language, it is imperative that you think not only about what you say but also about how you dress and behave.

Body language can be much louder than verbal communication. For example, if someone is holding a dormant position or arms crossed, we can assume that they are tired or uninterested in speech. If someone avoids eye contact, we may think it's because they have something to hide. None of the above may be true, but we must pay attention to how we behave; otherwise, people will perceive us negatively.

Here are eight simple tricks to perfecting the body language that can help people trust you.

Laugh... sincerely

This seems obvious, but the smiles that most of us use

daily are a bit fake. The key to a real smile is to smile with your eyes, to show your teeth when you smile, and to remove the smile from your face slowly. A real smile will make you more sincere, and therefore more reliable.

Lean forward

This mainly refers to leaning towards someone when sitting because you are showing attention and involvement in the conversation. When people feel that you are interested in them, it will make them more likely to trust you.

Look people in the eye

If you do not look people in the eye during the conversation, they may assume that you are not telling the truth, or that you are not completely sure of yourself or what you are saying. One should pretend that those eyes are glued to the partner you are talking to. Research shows that subjects significantly reported greater feelings of respect and affection for colleagues who used this technique.

Nodding

Nodding means agreeing with the person talking to you, which will make them more open. When you evoke this positive emotion, you are more likely to be trusted.

Point your toes when standing

Pointing your toes at someone means you are completely facing them. Nothing is more encouraging than someone who gives you full attention and consciously ignores other people and distractions to dedicate himself to talking to you. When your feet are pointing in the other direction, it sends the message that you are ready to go—and who would believe someone who always looks like he can't wait to "give in to the wind."

Keep your hands out of your pockets and visible

You don't want anyone to think you have something to hide, do you? Expert Katherine Noel states, "Make sure your hands are always visible, that you never hide them. Crossing your arms has a similar negative effect, making you look closed and unacceptable." Invite people and let them trust you using more open body language. Avoid positions that appear defensive.

Don't spin or squirm in place (but don't be too stiff)

A few signs that someone is lying are: they constantly move their feet, cover their mouths, and "wave" their hands. But we should also pay attention to those interlocutors whose bodies do not move at all. This can be a sign of a primitive neurological 'struggle' rather than an 'escape' from the response, as the body positions itself and prepares for possible conflicts. When you speak and participate in normal conversation, it is natural to move your body in subtle, relaxed, and mostly unconscious movements. So, if you observe the rigid, catatonic attitude of the interlocutor, without movement, it is often a huge warning sign that something is not right.

If you want people to trust you, relax.

Imitation of body language

This strategy is called mirroring (as mentioned before). When talking to someone, try to copy their body language, gestures, and facial expressions. Researchers from the University of New York documented the "chameleon effect" in 1999, which occurs when people unconsciously imitate others' behavior and that mimicry eases taste.

In the study, 78 men and women worked on a task with a partner. The partners dealt with different levels of mimicry, while the researchers secretly recorded the interactions. At the end of the interaction, the researchers and participants showed how much they liked those partners who mimicked their body language because they found them more harmonious and reliable.

CHAPTER 6

MASTERING THE SECRETS OF NON-VERBAL COMMUNICATION

Body language is hard to fake, but there are ways to learn to use positive body language while communicating with others and eliminate negative body language that can send the wrong message.

Most employers recognize communication as one of the basic skills that every employee must have and develop to adapt to the workplace's needs and expectations. We can communicate in various ways—orally, in writing, with movements, facial expressions, clothing, and the goal of every communication is the exchange of information, ideas, messages. In addition to giving and receiving information, ideas, or messages, an important part of successful communication is the interpretation of the same, i.e., whether the information, ideas, or messages are understood in the way and a sense intended by the sender. Like the same music, picture, or movie can produce different experiences for different people so that different people can understand the same message in different ways.

Manner of Transmission of The Message

In addition to the message's content, the way it is conveyed, and the context in which it takes place are also important. Nonverbal elements in speech such as voice tone, gaze, facial expression, gestures, body language, emotions (anger, happiness, fear, etc.) often cause the message to be misunderstood and seen more than we hear. Often due to uncoordinated verbal and non-verbal communication—when the interlocutor says one thing and his body language says something else—in some situations, we quickly realize that the interlocutor is saying one thing and thinking another and trying to "sell us a story" he does not believe.

As the folk saying goes: "One swallow does not make spring," so the true meaning of a gesture can have many different meanings if we look at it outside the context in which it takes place. One simple "scratching of the head," if we do not know the context in which it occurs, can be interpreted as a sign of lying, insecurity, forgetfulness, or that the interlocutor has "ears" or "dirty hair." Therefore, each gesture needs to be compared to other elements of nonverbal and verbal speech and placed in the context in which it occurs.

If at a bus stop, on a cold winter morning, you saw a person with his arms and legs tightly pressed and crossed and leaning against his body, with his head and chin pointing down—all these signs in this context would mean that the person is simply cold. But if you saw the same gestures on a person, you are in the same room with, in a meeting, and want to sell them a product or service, and you would correctly conclude that such gestures mean that the person feels negative or rejects your offer.

Strength of Hand and Palm

Throughout history, open hands and palms have been associated with openness, truth, fidelity, and honesty. Outstretched hands with palms facing the interlocutor send the message: "Trust me, I'm not lying." The palm facing up suggests that we are not a threat, that we are willing to listen, and that we want to talk. On the other hand, the palm facing downwards suggests authority and giving orders, and provokes opposition and rebellion in the interlocutor. The outstretched index finger creates a sense of threat and aggression and suggests the command: "Do it or otherwise...". The goal of the outstretched index finger is to obey the interlocutor and, as a rule, causes a negative reaction because we experience it as a physical attack. Interestingly, if we connect the index finger with the thumb, we send a message of thoughtfulness, focus, and goal orientation.

The first impression of a person at a meeting is usually obtained by shaking hands. It is important to know that the handshake sends subconscious messages, which, although we are not aware, can significantly affect the outcome of the meeting and our impression of the interlocutor. If we shake hands with the palm facing down, we send a message that we are taking control and that we are in charge. If we shake hands with the palm facing up, we send a message to obey the interlocutor and give him the feeling that he is in control of the situation.

What we should strive for when shaking hands is that

both interlocutors have their thumbs facing upward, which sends a message of equality. In addition to the palm's position, it is important always to apply the same grip force we get (so if our grip is stronger, we should give in, if it's weaker, we need to squeeze harder). The nonverbal messages sent by our body are a key part of our communication and are often even more important than what we say.

Communication skills, both verbal and non-verbal, are extremely important in human relationships because unsuccessful communication creates numerous misunderstandings, problems, and conflicts. In contrast, successful communication improves interpersonal relationships and contributes to a true understanding of the interlocutor.

Some interesting facts about hands:

Many people cannot lie convincingly if their palms are open to the interlocutor because gestures and feelings are directly related.

When we speak with our palms open to the interlocutor, we create pressure on the interlocutor, to be honest with us.

If we keep our arms crossed on our chests while listening to the interlocutor, we will begin to feel a defensive attitude.

Research has shown that 84% of listeners respond positively to content if the speaker holds their palms facing up, 52% if the speaker holds their palms facing down, and only 28% if the speaker uses an outstretched index finger.

How to Interpret Verbal Communication

Even being far from each other, people communicate. There are several ways to express your thoughts and get acquainted with a stranger. In psychology, this is called verbal and non-verbal communication. The first of them is the most accessible and understandable to others.

Verbal Communication in Psychology

The deaf and dumb also speak, but through gestures. You can speak out by changing the position of the body, facial expressions, eyes. These are all ways of non-verbal contact.

Verbal communication is the transmission and receipt of information through speech (it does not matter whether it is oral or written). All people do not understand sign language, but the sign system using words is available to most.

As a child, a person learns to communicate using speech as the most accessible and understandable way to express his desires and convey important information to his interlocutor. The phrases expressed aloud are more obvious than attempts to explain something with gestures. The power of the word helps the interlocutors to hear and understand each other.

Without verbal communication, a person feels closed in the "shell of loneliness." The lack of communication skills will not make it possible to learn the world, improve, and reach certain heights.

Speech has several features that allow people to interact with each other. These characteristics emphasize the importance of communication.

The components of verbal communication

<u>Name Features</u>

Total: Even communicating at a distance (by phone), you can get some information about the person you are talking to by voice, intonation, and said phrases: gender, approximate age, temperament, state of health, etc.

Personal: Any conversation evokes emotions, attuning to positive contact, or provokes indignation. With some, you want to communicate with others, and it is better to end the conversation immediately.

Emotional: Communication is a way of self-expression, an opportunity for harmonious development. Information can be obtained from books, textbooks, television. Mutual communication helps to get emotions, find a response to your feelings and thoughts.

Common preferences among people around or different views on life - this does not prevent them from contacting each other. Speech helps build relationships (family, neighborhood, production) and is a tool to achieve your own goals.

How verbal communication is used

Verbal speech is called a symbolic communication system in which the meaning of a transmitted or received message is not lost. It is based on two principles:

- Set of words of a particular language (this is vocabulary).
- Rules for creating units of speech (syntax).
- Non-verbal communication - what is it in psychology.

In psychology, speech and thinking are inseparable, because the first is a form of existence of the second. When people communicate with each other, this happens according to this scheme:

- The speaker mentally selects certain words.
- Using the rules of vocabulary and syntax forms phrases from them.
- Only then pronounces them out loud.
- The interlocutor decodes the information for mental perception and creates images in his head.

Note! Even with the clear transmission of information, distortions and semantic losses are possible, amounting to about 60%.

If the proposal were made according to the rules of grammar, communication difficulties would not arise. But only if people speak a language that is understandable to each other.

How to reach an interlocutor

The same applies to writing. To get information from print media (or at least read SMS), a person must know this language. To state your thoughts on paper (type text on the keyboard), you need to not only be able to speak, but also write.

Spoken or written words help to analyze objects, events, and phenomena, to find the main and secondary signs in them. Bare, concrete facts are inherent in business speech. For emotional contact, additional verbal means are needed:

- Voice modulation, intonation, pauses, rhythm in oral speech.
- The range of handwriting, and the angle of inclination, the pressure, and direction of the lines in the letter.

These expressive characteristics make it possible to understand how the correspondent himself relates to the message and the person he communicates with.

Types of Verbal Communication

Why is communication necessary for a person—what does it give, and why is it important for people?

Verbal means of communication is speech, which inaction is divided into two types: "say-listen," "write-read." In other words, speech is divided into oral and written. Each of them, in turn, is divided into components.

Speech Types

Name Definition

- **Oral:**

Dialogue: A consistent change in the roles of communicating individuals, in the speech of which there is a certain meaning, is characteristic. By exchanging phrases, the interlocutors make it clear to each other that they understand the essence of what the recipient said.

Monologue: A lengthy statement by one person that is not interrupted by others (for example, a lecture, a report, a campaign speech, a presentation of a product, etc.)

- **Written:**

Direct: Correspondence in real-time is carried out through SMS messages, the exchange of notes in the lesson, etc.

Delayed: Communication via paper or email.

There is another kind of speech—dactyl, which is used by blind and deaf-mute people. The signs used in it are a manual alphabet that replaces the usual letters.

Oral and written speech is classified as external, the existence of which is unrealistic without internal speech. It is formed in the head of a person before an individual voices it out or writes it.

Language and its functions

Types of communication in psychology - what applies to them, its functions.

Language does not just express the thoughts and feelings of people. It is impossible to imagine any aspect of life wherever speech is applied.

Language features

Name Definition

Communicative: It provides interaction between people, allowing you to communicate with your kind fully.

Accumulative: The ability to accumulate and store knowledge, passing it on to descendants (notebooks, abstracts, fiction, and scientific literature).

Cognitive: Language helps to gain knowledge from books, films, scientific treatises, lectures, etc.

Constructive: It makes it possible to put thought into an accessible, understandable to others conscious form in the form of written or verbal expression.

Ethnic: It unites people not only in groups of the same nationality. Through language, communication is possible between the peoples of the whole world.

Emotional: With the help of words you can convey to your interlocutor your feelings and emotions.

To successfully use the functions of language in one's own life, a person must learn to communicate and build relationships. The ability to speak is influenced by knowledge of one's own and foreign languages, the rules of speech production, as well as the mental aspect. Fear of contact with other individuals interferes with some people in communication. Inaction only exacerbates the situation.

Rules for verbal communication

To achieve the desired result in the development of relations, it is necessary to take into account some points and apply them in practice:

- It is necessary to show goodwill and respect for the interlocutor.
- Do not impose your point of view on the issues discussed and tactfully circumvent the "sharp corners".
- Observe logic in statements and consistency in conversation.
- Build a conversation on brief lines and the optimal amount of information.
- Present truthful information relevant to the subject of the conversation.
- Take into account the nationality, social status, and attitude of the interlocutor in the communication.

In the dialogue, it is important to observe the sequence of statements. A person who interrupts the speaker for no reason emphasizes the low level of his speech culture by such behavior.

How to make verbal communication effective

Thanks to communication, people coexist in this world, achieving certain heights in life. For communications to give positive results, and those around you want to communicate with a specific person, you must adhere to several principles:

- By his attention and interest, arouse a strong desire in the opponent to communicate.
- Sincerely and honestly evaluate people and events.
- Do not complain, condemn, or criticize.
- Show interest in the interlocutor, talk about things important to him.
- Learning not only to clearly state your thoughts but also to listen carefully to the opponent's speech.

Important! A thought that is clumsily expressed may be misinterpreted. But inattentive listening distorts the meaning of the information received. The ability to speak and listen are two components of communicative communication.

Interest in the interlocutor

It is important not only what they say, but also how the words are pronounced. For the interlocutor, the emotions and para verbal signals (articulation, speed, tonality, and accompanying sounds) present in the speech can mean more than the phrases said.

Some people can think clearly but are not able to formulate phrases in oral speech. Others speak well, but they are difficult to put into writing. Or vice versa — beautifully set out on paper, but in verbal communication tongue-tied.

To achieve harmony in all verbal speech versions, you need to improve your abilities and overcome psychological barriers.

What do languages have in common?

A person in life uses two types of communication. Non-verbal language is not the prerogative of the deaf-mute. It can be called an external manifestation of brain activity. Not having begun to utter phrases out loud, an individual with facial expressions, body posture, and gaze can unwittingly hint about the course of his thoughts.

But the interlocutor may incorrectly interpret such signals, or the individual intentionally distorts the information transmitted by body language. To understand the partner and get complete information, the analysis also requires voice contact.

Verbal speech and body language in harmony

So that communication does not tire the partner, both languages must be balanced. Monotony, emotionless speech, excessive gestures interfere with the perception of information and can alienate the interlocutor.

A misunderstanding leads not only to disappointment in relationships but also to serious conflicts. This is manifested at any level: in the family, business, and business communication, thereby complicating life. Having learned to speak body language and verbal, bringing both types of communication into harmony, a person will achieve great success in any field.

Verbal and non-verbal communication - what is it

Verbally - this word comes from the Latin "verbalis," which means verbally. Communication, in this case, occurs through words.

Verbal communication is of three types:

- Speech - communication through words (dialogues, monologues).
- Written communication - by hand, printing on a computer, SMS, etc.
- Inner - your inner dialogue (the formation of thoughts).

Nonverbal - other types of communication, except verbal. What could it be:

- Gestures, facial expressions, and postures - all this tells us a lot if you can read them.
- Visual - scanning a person in the first seconds when you see him: determining sex, age, assessing the appearance, and facial expression.
- Acoustic non-verbal perception is an assessment of the voice (its rhythm, timbre, volume, brightness, pauses, cough, parasite words).
- Tactile non-verbal communication - touch (it is very significant).
- Smells - some attract, and some repel.
- Mobility - enlivens perception, but if mobility is too high, fatigue occurs.
- The boundaries of personal space - their transition takes a person out of the comfort zone or, conversely, brings them closer together.

Verbally is our difference from another living world

Words that are compiled into speech are a unit of our communication with others. We use them both in oral pronunciation and writing. Or typing (typing on the keyboard), if we talk about realities that are closer to us. Such communication is divided depending on who plays what role: speak - listen, write - read.

To maintain verbal communication at a high level, it is necessary to develop its components. This is, first of all, vocabulary (what is it?). Reading books, listening to vocabulary, talking with intellectually developed people - all this greatly helps to replenish and expand vocabulary.

In written communication, it is important to know the rules of punctuation to present the information correctly. Often, by incorrectly placing dots and commas, you can distort the meaning or focus on something wrong. We all remember the cartoon where you had to put the punctuation mark in the right way and save your life: "You can't have mercy on execution."

Speech and written communication solve several problems at once:

- Communicative - provides interaction between people in its large-scale manifestations.
- Cognitive - a person receives knowledge and new information.
- Accumulative - display of accumulated knowledge (writing abstracts, books).
- Emotional - you can express your attitude to the

world, feelings using words.
- Ethnic - an association of the populations of different countries (in the language used).

Forms of verbal communication and barriers are not one way

Communicating verbally, we can use different forms and styles to convey certain information in a specific context and color. This can be well traced by the styles used in literature:

- Journalistic - the main goal of such a speech is to convey to people the idea, the essence of what happened.
- Scientific - different logic and clear statements using terminology, complex concepts.
- Official business is a dry language of laws, where everything is accurate and without any epithets.
- Artistic - a combination of any words and word forms, jargon, and dialect (dialectism) is possible here; speech is filled with unimaginable images and colors.
- Conversational - characterizes both individual dialogues in works and our communication with others or when we meet a friend.

Speech interaction can be divided by the number of people who take part in this:

- Monologue (one person).
- Performance - in meetings in front of someone or reciting a verse in front of the class.

- Report - important information, as a rule, is supported by figures.
- Statement - similar to a report but provides more extensive information and description.
- Lecture - providing useful information to the audience.

Dialogue (two or more people):

- Ordinary conversation - exchange of greetings and thoughts.
- Discussion - a discussion of the topic where the interlocutors act as representatives of different points of view.
- Dispute - here, too, there are two positions between which you need to resolve the resulting conflict.
- A dispute is a discussion within the framework of science.
- Interview - a conversation during which the employer considers whether it is worth hiring a person.

Even though we communicate in the same language, various barriers to verbal communication may arise:

For example, phonetic. The interlocutor may have a speech impediment, unpleasant diction, pick up unusual intonation, sprinkle with words parasites, etc...

The semantic noise grows between people from different countries, with a different mentality or even when raising children in different families.

The logical barrier is that the interlocutors have different types of thinking, levels of development, and intelligence.

The stylistic barrier is that the interlocutor incorrectly builds a chain of verbal communication to convey information. First, we need to draw attention to what we want to say to interest. Then lay out the basic information; answer questions that the opponent may have. After that, give time to think so that he draws conclusions or makes a decision.

Non-verbal communication - we inherited it

Non-verbal communication is body language (as in the rest of the animal world). Facial expressions, gestures, poses, touches. As well as visual and acoustic perception, smells, distance, and movement of communicating objects—all exactly like animals.

All this can carry a lot of information, so do not neglect this format to impress people (with a pleasant perfume and appearance, set by voice and manner of movement).

It is important not only to interpret these signals correctly but also to send them correctly to the interlocutor. Non-verbal communication is not only an addition to the conversation using words but can completely replace it in some situations.

Accents - this is something that can be successfully placed using non-verbal means if you cannot do it in full intonation. After all, it is often necessary to indicate to the interlocutor that you think what you focus your attention on is important. So that background information does not take much time for analysis and decision making.

Sadness, anger, joy, sadness, satisfaction - this is what can best be emphasized by verbal means (you can even completely show these feelings with your gestures and facial expressions). Therefore, if you are attentive to the interlocutor, you can read his condition without words.

The distance between the interlocutors can also be analyzed. The closer they are, the more they trust each other.

Differences between types of communication

Communication with words is characteristic exclusively for people because it requires a strong development of the brain. Other animals are not capable of this. But non-verbal signals send absolutely everything.

If a cat wags its tail — it is unhappy, if a dog does the same — it experiences joyful emotions. It turns out that even at the level of animals, you need to be able to correctly interpret the signs they give, given who exactly is standing in front of you. What can you see if you are facing different people?

It is worth noting that sign language is more sincere since we have almost no control over it. Therefore, it is so easy to deceive a person by phone or correspondence. But if a fraudster tries to do this while standing in front of you, then there is a chance that you will read through his facial expressions that he should not be trusted.

We are people, which means that both types of communication (verbal and non-verbal) are open to us, so you should use them to the maximum for your purposes. This is a great tool to achieve what you want and get everything you need from life.

Verbal communication: definition, types, and principles

COMMUNICATION (English communication, intercourse, interpersonal relationship) - the interaction of 2 or more people, consisting of the exchange between them of information of a cognitive and affective-evaluative nature.

Verbal communication - uses human speech as a sign system, natural sound language, a system of phonetic signs that includes two principles: lexical and syntactic. Speech is the most versatile means of communication because the transmission of information through speech is less unlikely to lose the meaning of the message.

The system of phonetic signs of the language is based on vocabulary and syntax. Vocabulary is a collection of words that make up a language. The syntax is a language-specific means and rule for creating speech units.

Speech is the universal means of communication because when transmitting information, the meaning of the message is lost to the least extent compared to other means of transmitting the information. Thus, speech is a language in action, a form of generalized reflection of reality, a form of thinking.

Indeed, in thinking, speech is manifested in the form of an internal pronunciation of words to oneself. Thinking and speech are not separable from each other.

The recipient (listener) perceives speech and decodes the speech units to understand the thoughts expressed in it correctly. But this happens when the communicants use a national language that is understandable to both developed in the process of verbal communication over many generations of people.

Speech performs two main functions - significative and communicative.

Thanks to the signifying function for a person (unlike an animal), it becomes possible to arbitrarily call up images of objects and perceive the semantic content of speech. Thanks to the communicative function, speech becomes a means of communication, a means of transmitting the information.

Words make it possible to analyze objects, things, and highlight significant and secondary signs of them. Mastering words, a person automatically masters complex systems of connections and relations between objects and phenomena of the objective world.

A dictionary compiled on this basis, encompassing terms and concepts of a special field of activity, is called a thesaurus.

The communicative function of speech is manifested in the means of expression and means of influence.

Speech is not limited to the totality of transmitted messages. It expresses both the person's attitude to what he is talking about and his attitude to the person he communicates.

Expressive components are also available in written speech (in the text of the letter). This is manifested in the range of handwriting and the force of pressure, the angle of its inclination, the direction of the lines, and the shape of capital letters, etc. The word as a means of influence and its emotional and expressive components are inextricable and act simultaneously, to a certain extent affecting the recipient's behavior.

Types of Verbal Communication

Distinguish between external and internal speech. External speech is divided into oral and written. Oral speech, in turn, is dialogic and monologic.

In preparing for the oral speech, and especially for writing, the individual "speaks" the speech to himself. This is inner speech. In written language, the conditions for communication are mediated by text.

Written speech can be direct (for example, the exchange of notes at a meeting, at a lecture) or delayed (exchange of letters).

A peculiar form of verbal communication is dactyl speech. This is a manual alphabet that serves to replace spoken language when deaf and blind people and people familiar with fingerprinting communicate among themselves. Fingerprints replace letters (similar to letters in print).

The accuracy of the listener's understanding of the

meaning of the speaker's statement depends on feedback. Such feedback is established when the communicator and the recipient are interchanged. Through his statement, the recipient makes it clear how he understood the meaning of the information received. Thus, dialogue speech is a kind of sequential change in the communicative roles of communicating, during which the meaning of the speech message is revealed. Monologue, the same speech, lasts long enough, and is not interrupted by replicas of others. It requires preliminary preparation. This is usually a detailed, preparatory speech (for example, a report, lecture, etc.).

Constant and effective exchange of information is the key to achieving any organization or firm's goals. The importance of verbal communication, for example, in management, cannot be overestimated.

However, it is necessary to pursue the goal of ensuring the correct understanding of the transmitted information or semantic messages. The ability to accurately express one's thoughts and the ability to listen are the components of the communicative side of communication. An inept expression of thoughts leads to a misinterpretation of what has been said.

Ineffective listening distorts the meaning of the transmitted information.

The main functions of the language in the communication process include: communicative (information exchange function); constructive (formulation of thoughts);

appellate (impact on the addressee); emotional (direct emotional reaction to the situation); fatal (exchange of ritual (etiquette) formulas); metalanguage (interpretation function. It is used if necessary, to check whether the interlocutors use the same code).

Thanks to the observation of non-verbal means of communication, we can draw a huge amount of information about our partner.

Verbal communication is "the process of establishing and maintaining purposeful, direct or indirect contact between people using language" (V. Kunitsyna, 2001, p. 46).

According to the authors of the book "Interpersonal Communication" (ibid.), talking people can have speech flexibility to varying degrees. So, some of them pay minimal attention to the choice of speech means, talking at different times with different people, in different circumstances, mainly in the same style.

Others, trying to maintain their stylistic appearance, can perform different speech roles, using a diverse style speech repertoire in various situations. However, in addition to the participants' characteristics in verbal communication, the social context influences the choice of the style of speech behavior.

The role-playing situation dictates the need to turn to poetic, then to the official, or scientific or everyday speech.

In cases of conflict with parents, it is better to adhere to the official manner of communication.

The principle of cooperation "the requirement for the interlocutors to act in a manner that would correspond to the accepted goal and direction of the conversation" - suggests that verbal communication should:

- Contain the Optimal Amount of Information. (It Should Correspond to The Current Goals of Communication, Redundant Information Can Be Distracting, Misleading).
- Contain Truthful Statements.
- Correspond to Goals, Subject of Conversation.
- Be Clear (Avoid Obscure Expressions, verbosity).

The principle of politeness, which implies expression in speech:

- Tact.
- Generosity.
- Endorsement.
- Modesty.
- Consent.
- Benevolence.

Pedagogical practice shows that an incorrectly built verbal message can lead to both partners not understanding each other and to open conflict.

That is why the literature devoted to the problems of constructive behavior in conflict is aimed at optimizing verbal communication (Grishina N.V., 2002).

Verbal communication

Verbal communication is a communicative, mutually directed action that occurs between one individual, several subjects, or more, which involves the transmission of information of a different orientation and its reception. In verbal communicative interaction, speech is used as a communication mechanism, which is represented by language systems and is divided into written and oral. The most important verbal communication requirement is the clarity of pronunciation, clarity of content, and accessibility of thought presentation.

Verbal communication can trigger a positive or negative emotional response. That is why each individual simply needs to know and correctly apply the rules, norms, and techniques of verbal interaction. For communication efficiency and success in life, anyone should master the art of rhetoric.

Verbal and nonverbal communication

As you know, the human individual is a social being. That is, the subject can never become a person without society. The interaction of subjects with society occurs through communication tools (communication), verbal and non-verbal.

Verbal and non-verbal means of communication provide a communicative interaction of individuals around the world.

Although a person has primary thought, for its expression and understanding by other individuals, such an instrument of verbal communication as speech is needed, which convicts thoughts.

The universal means of communication between people is the language, which is the main system encoding information, and an important tool for communication.

With the help of words, a person clarifies the meaning of events and the meaning of phenomena and expresses his thoughts, feelings, positions, and worldview. Personality, language, and consciousness are inseparable. However, in this case, the vast majority of people relate to language as they do to air, i.e., use it without noticing. Language quite often overtakes thoughts or does not obey them.

During the communication of people at each stage, barriers arise that impede the effectiveness of communication.

Individual differences in human needs and their system of values often do not make it possible to find a common language even when discussing universal topics.

Violations of the process of communication human interaction cause errors, mistakes, or failures in encrypting information, underestimation of worldview, professional, ideological, religious, political, age, and gender differences.

Also, the following factors are incredibly important for human communications: context, subtext, and style. For example, an unexpected familiar appeal or cheeky behavior can nullify the entire informational richness of the conversation.

That is, the idea of the interlocutor's true feelings and intentions, the subjects derive not from his speech, but with direct observation of the details and manner of his behavior.

In other words, interpersonal communication interaction is mainly carried out thanks to a whole range of non-verbal instruments—facial expressions and gestures, symbolic communicative signs, spatial and temporal boundaries, intonational and rhythmic characteristics of speech.

Verbal and non-verbal means of communication in the course of communication between people are perceived simultaneously; they should be considered as a single complex. Also, gestures without the use of speech are not always consistent, and speech without facial expressions is empty.

Types of Verbal Communication

Verbal communication refers to externally directed speech, divided into written and oral, and internally directed speech. Oral speech can be dialogic or monologic. Inner speech is manifested in preparation for a conversation or, especially, for written speech.

Writing is direct and delayed. Direct speech occurs during the exchange of notes, for example, at a meeting or lecture, and delayed speech occurs during the exchange of letters, which can take quite a long time to get an answer. The conditions of communication in writing are strictly mediated by text.

It follows that dialogue speech is a sequential change in the roles of communicative interaction of the conversation, in the process of which the meaning of speech utterance is revealed. On the contrary, a monologue speech can last quite a while, not interrupting other conversants. It requires prior preparation from the speaker.

Monological speech includes lectures, reports, etc.

Important components of the communicative aspect of communication are the ability to express their thoughts and listening skills accurately. Since the fuzzy formulation of thoughts leads to an incorrect interpretation of the spoken. And inept listening transforms the meaning of the broadcast information.

The well-known type of interaction is also related to verbal communication—conversation, interview, disputes and discussions, debates, meetings, etc.

Participants in the conversation can ask each other questions to familiarize themselves with the interlocutor's position or clarify incomprehensible points that arose during the discussion. A conversation is especially effective when it becomes necessary to clarify a question or to highlight a problem. An interview is a specially organized conversation on social, professional, or scientific topics.

A dispute is a public discussion or debate on a socially important or scientific topic. A discussion is called a public dispute, the result of which is the clarification and correlation of various points of view, positions, search and identification of the correct opinion, finding the right solution to the controversial issue. The dispute is called the process of exchanging opposing views.

That is, it denotes any clash of positions, disagreements in beliefs and views, a kind of struggle in which each of the participants defends its innocence.

Interpersonal communication is carried out between several individuals, the result of which is the emergence of psychological contact and a certain relationship between communicating.

Verbal business communication is a complex multilateral process of developing contacts between people in the professional sphere.

Features of verbal communication

The main feature of verbal communication is that such communication is peculiar only to man. Verbal communication as an indispensable condition involves mastering the language.

Due to its communicative potential, it is much richer than all types of non-verbal communication, although it is not able to completely replace it.

The formation of verbal communications initially necessarily relies on non-verbal means of communication.

Any message built using a non-verbal sign system can be decrypted or translated into verbal human language.

So, for example, the red light of a traffic light can be translated as "no traffic" or "stop."

The verbal aspect of communication has a complex multi-level structure and can appear in different stylistic variations: dialect, spoken and literary language, etc. All speech components or other characteristics facilitate the successful or unsuccessful implementation of a communicative act.

Such a process is endless in its diversity

Words in verbal communicative interaction are not ordinary signs that serve to name objects or phenomena. In verbal communication, entire verbal complexes, systems of ideas, religions, myths characteristic of a particular society or culture are created and formed.

The way the subject speaks can form another participant's idea in the interaction about who such a subject is.

This often occurs when the communicator plays an established social role, such as the head of the company, the school director, the team captain, etc.

The choice of verbal tools contributes to the creation and comprehension of certain social situations. So, for example, a compliment will not always indicate that a person looks good; it can simply be a kind of "communicative move."

The effectiveness and efficiency of verbal interaction are largely due to the level of communicator's mastery of oratory and its qualitative characteristics. Today, proficiency in speech is considered the most important component of the professional realization of a person.

With the help of speech, not only the movement of messages takes place, but also the interaction of the participants in the communication process, which is a special way to influence each other, direct and orient each other. In other words, they strive to achieve a certain transformation of behavior.

How to Influence and Subdue Anyone's Mind

Having the full mastery of communication skills to defend ideas and present your point of view to others is a fundamental characteristic for anyone who wants to know how to influence people—especially in the business world. After all, people tend to trust those who demonstrate security in their beliefs deeply. Because of this, when a manager is unable to communicate effectively—nor sustain his speeches for a long time—we can perceive the negative impacts on results and organizational influence. In such situations, employees are likely not willing to experience what the leader propagates, which generates enormous institutional disorder. With that in mind, we have prepared this section to teach you some tips on how to influence people through simple, practical tips. Read on to find out how this is possible!

1. Know how to give and receive feedback—on any issue—whether positive or negative. It is essential to keep employees motivated and aligned with the organization and the team's performance. However, for this tip to be useful when influencing people, it is necessary to know the correct way to give feedback. To give assertive feedback, it is important to reflect on the relevance and integrity of what is going to be said, as well as to maintain a concise and direct communication. It is essential to recognize what is well done and give tips to improve behavior or performance. After that, carefully follow the case to see if the requested changes have occurred or if it will be necessary to intervene again in the process.

2. Treat everyone by name. One of the most practical ways to open efficient communication channels and get closer to the interlocutors is to refer to everyone involved. After all, it is the key piece of personal identity. Using it to refer to someone, you will certainly be able to create much greater intimacy and keep others interested in what you have to say. On the other hand, it is necessary to pay attention to excessive nicknames or that demonstrate proximity that does not exist between you and the listener. Do not forget that professionalism should be the focus of communication.

3. Mirror behaviors. This type of conduct—known as "mimicry"—is capable of making the person whose movements are mirrored more likely to act positively towards the person who imitates him. This is because the human being has an inherent tendency to sympathize with those who look or act similarly to him. It is a type of behavior that few people naturally adopt without realizing it. However, through good observation and a lot of training, it is possible to develop this skill and use it to influence people. Over time, it will become spontaneous.

4. Demonstrate proactivity. If you want to learn how to influence people, it is important to understand that, in general, we all have a real inclination to admire and follow those who are good examples. This is where proactivity comes in, based on self-responsibility and anticipating needs or problems. You probably have already realized that the most proactive employees are the most admired and, consequently, the most respected, right? With that in mind, don't forget to always be proactive in the workplace. As a result, you will inspire and influence more people.

5. Invest in emotional balance. Maintaining the balance of emotions in the workplace is a challenge for many employees in the market. The lack of this capacity, however, can cause several problems and also hinder corporate interpersonal relationships. To achieve the desired balance, it is necessary to develop emotional intelligence. With that, it will be possible to identify and control your emotions assertively. The good news is that there are several behavioral trainings to improve and make that ability flourish. What are you waiting for to start developing this skill?

6. Give praise. It seems obvious. But the truth is that many people do not take advantage of the potential that good praise has to offer for the art of influence. A lot of people don't know when and how to praise—let alone how to make it not feel forced. And this is exactly where our 6th tip comes in. Thus, when praising someone, be careful that the praise is really sincere, after all, the intention is to validate what the person feels about you and not create a doubt about the truth of what was said. By doing this—without exaggeration or flattery—you are sure to make the speaker more likely to accept what you say. Incredible, isn't it?

7. Plan strategic approaches. Applied to the previous tips, it is time to plan how you will present your ideas so that the listeners will accept them. Planning is very important in this process and must go hand in hand with those who want to learn how to influence people. Therefore, it is essential to develop a script for your approach and rehearse the best way to present it.

Also, be sure to prepare yourself for any questions that may arise and schedule convincing responses to avoid being taken by surprise. Knowing the importance of following the tips presented, it is interesting to note that good behavioral training can be a key piece in influencing people. Do not forget to look for a company that has experience and recognition in the market. Otherwise, you may lose time and money.

CHAPTER 7

HOW TO USE SUBLIMINAL MESSAGES TO MANIPULATE

Subliminal messages are emitted at a level below the limit of human perception so that the human eye cannot perceive them in time, which means that they cannot become aware of the brain due to their brevity.

Influence of subliminal messages on the brain

They usually appear in the duration of three-hundredths of 30 milliseconds in the form of words or pictures. This type of message stimulates different parts of the human brain, especially the area of vision important for perceiving shapes, colors and movements, as well as the temporal lobe, which is responsible for memory and object recognition, and the limbic system in which emotions are created. Even though they stimulate many areas in the brain, these three-hundredths are still not enough to leave an effect on the frontal lobe in charge of raising awareness of all these previously mentioned colors and shapes.

Most of today's films are made so that thirty pictures are placed in every second of the shot, which means that each picture lasts three hundredths. This leads us to the conclusion that constantly watching such moving content, we are stimulated in various ways. We are not aware.

Producers and filmmakers use this method. It is also known that subliminal messages can be read from cartoons, such as those of the Warner brothers, in one with the famous character Duck Dodd, in a split second a shield of a metal figure appears in which engraved letters say "buy bonds", encouraging Americans to support the financing of the war. Such messages try to instill a certain intention in the subconscious part of the human mind. In the last few decades, this method is very popular. However, today it has become common to pause movies or videos whenever we want so that these same subliminal messages can still be made aware in some way. Interestingly, products sell better if they have some hidden meaning related to sexuality, but of course, such inappropriate images or words are not noticed at first glance.

Chronology of conducted experiments

In 1957, there was great interest in America in the idea of subliminal messages. Namely, at that time, James Vicary appeared to be a market researcher who began to deal with the concept of advertising through this method seriously. He experimented by inserting subliminal messages into the films, such as, "Are you hungry? Buy popcorn." Or "Are you thirsty? Drink Coca-Cola." also lasting three hundredths. After experimenting, Vicary said sales of popcorn and especially Coca-Cola had increased significantly. After that, he became a kind of marketing guru, and he was invited to television and radio shows where he spoke about the successful results of the freshly tried method. At the end of his career, he earned a total of $4 million at the time on his very idea, which would be $36 million.

In addition to the great interest in the new concept, a mass hysteria arose from the question of how much power and influence subliminal messages can have. A Cold War period soon followed, and Westerners thought that Russia might be interfering with American television waves and injecting messages like "Kill the President." This is why the US government's Federal Communications Commission (FCC) received a handful of complaints and letters from concerned citizens in the 1970s, to which it replied that it would investigate and report any such cases, for which there is no evidence or record—cases in which a person is sought or sued who could abuse the idea of subliminal messages.

The panic that spread seemed unnecessary because James Vicary himself denied the success of his experiment, stating that he had invented it. He said that the instructions he inserted about buying popcorn did not affect the increased sale of popcorn. Also, the scientists who later tried to conduct Vicary's experiment again did not get the results he first claimed to have obtained. This concept may have no power of influence, but since it is intriguing, it has continued to be discussed and researched, and ultimately proved that in certain circumstances it could have a certain influence on man.

In 2002, the true power of messages and images displayed in a short time began to be explored. This research was conducted by psychologists Erin Strahan, Steven Spencer, and Mark Zanna. They wanted to prove whether messages inserted into the subconscious can make people thirsty. James Vicary himself said that showing messages derived from the word thirst can make people feel subjective thirst and increase the likelihood of buying drinks. To experiment, they gathered a group of people to whom they displayed words such as thirsty, dry, and dehydrated. In doing so, the respondents had to concentrate on the center of the screen.

The research showed that the messages displayed on the screen had almost no effect on the group that came to the interrogation and they did not feel thirsty. The turnaround happened with the part of the group that came to the interrogation already a little thirsty and who were told not to drink anything for the next three hours. The results of research in this part of the group showed that subliminal messages had a very large impact on emphasizing and intensifying the feeling of thirst. As a reward, all respondents received a glass of juice at the end of the study, which was also part of the experiment because this is how the strength of thirst was tested, so some already thirsty people drank much more than the other part.

A few years later, in 2006, psychologists Johan C. Karremans, Wolfgang Stroebe, and Jasper Claus came up with the assumption that subliminal messages can amplify a particular feeling such as thirst but can affect people in terms of standing behind a particular producer. As an example, Lipton iced tea was used for the experiment. The researchers used part of the 2002 study by dividing the respondents into two groups; in one, the respondents were thirsty, and in the other, they were not. Also, as in the previous study, respondents were required to focus on the central part of the screen on which the Lipton logos were displayed separately within three-hundredths of a second.

And pictures of their iced tea. At the end of the experiment, the researchers offered the subjects two types of iced tea, one of which was Lipton, and the other iced tea was from an unknown manufacturer. It has been proven that already thirsty respondents preferred Lipton iced tea. It can be said that this 2006 survey served as a complement to the 2002 one, proving that subliminal messages can not only amplify a particular feeling but have the power to steer people in a particular direction to meet their unmet needs.

In 2013, psychologists Bryan Gibson and Katherine Zielaskowski researched a Las Vegas casino where they inserted thumbnails showing a US dollar symbol or a jackpot message on second-hand clips on slot machines. What followed is very interesting, and that is that some of the people who were shown these messages invested 55% more money on gambling and betting than other people in the casino. And as many as 45% of people after the bombardment of messages and the pictures were convinced that they would win something. Their mind interpreted that message as a sure win, an incentive to invest even more, and simply, as support for the opinion with which they had already come to the casino, and that is that there is a possibility of winning something and multiplying their money.

The question is, is there any protection against these cunning, flashing influences? Of course, certain agencies try to prevent subliminal messages from spreading through television and radio to viewers and listeners, but as soon as we step into a mall, casino, or any place intended for consumers, agencies do not influence because the owners of such places determine what to do. How to present to your consumers. One should be prepared for the fact that by going to any store, we will be exposed to subliminal messages. Lately, it is fashionable to show products on small screens, even in the nearest stores where we go to get basic groceries. The more technology develops, the more information is available to retailers about what consumers want.

On this occasion, it is convenient to say that one should never make decisions hungry, as it is not wise to go shopping hungry. If our needs, especially the primary, physiological ones, are not met, we are in great exposure to subliminal messages from various manufacturers. Just because all we have in mind is hunger or thirst, we won't even think about being exposed to commercials. The stroller gets piled up, and then, when we get full and watered, we realize that we probably don't need so many purchased things.

CHAPTER 8

HOW THE EYES CAN TELL US A LOT OF THINGS

Are you satisfied with your ability to communicate with people? Few will answer this question with a confident yes. More often than not, we only talk about how it will turn out and how it develops spontaneously on its own. And that means—we risk achieving a result that we did not want and did not expect at all. It happens, however, that we prepare in advance for a complex, responsible conversation. But even then, as experience shows, it is not easy to point it in the right direction towards the desired goal. Of course, some lucky people have such talent from birth. Well, if you are not one of them, try using the NLP technique.

To learn the skills of "effective" communication, a person must learn how to follow the course of their mental processes, to recognize emotional states, to assess the sincerity of statements, and the degree of agreement or disagreement with them.

First of all, you need to understand how the interlocutor's mind "processes" your words and prepares an answer. The first assistant here will be the method of observing the direction of a person's gaze. Summarizing and analyzing the vast amount of experimental material, the creators of NLP were convinced of the surprising informativeness and reliability of this simple feature.

In previous chapters it has already been said that according to the theory of NLP the human consciousness is connected with the external world and with its subconscious through three systems of sensations, images and notions: visual (sight), auditory (sound) and kinesthetic (muscular sensations, taste, odor). You can find out which of these systems is most active at the moment, what experiences the person now has.

The eyes are the mirror of the soul... It is unlikely to understand how real this old aphorism is. For example, clearly manifested in sight, even just in the direction of one's eyes, is the hidden structure of our inner world.

What do we do by orienting ourselves in the surrounding space or looking for the right object? Expressing ourselves not too intelligently, but very precisely, we shine with our eyes. But in the end, inner contemplation, the search for the right image, word, idea is said very similarly: "wander with the eye of your mind." And so—it turned out that this is not a metaphor at all! In such cases, we are looking at a very real, albeit very unusual, space arrangement.

On the one hand, it has a meaningful, "semantic" structure—it is divided into zones corresponding to three systems of representation (visual, auditory, and kinesthetic). On the other hand, these areas in our consciousness, for some reason, are tied to strictly defined directions of external, physical space. And the connection is so strong that any mental representation appeals to any area.

According to the scheme given in the book by NLP creators John Grinder and Richard Bandler, "From Frogs to Princes," six main lines of vision have the following semantic content.

Centuries (look to the left) - visual memories. This is an area of visual images of those objects that one has already seen once. For example, questions such as, "What color are your wife's eyes?" "What does your house look like?"

Bk (lookup) - visual constructions. Visual images of those things or phenomena that one has never seen or never seen in the way one should imagine. Typical questions: "What will an orange cow with blue spots look like?" "What will you look like in a firefighter's suit?"

AB (left side view) - audio memories. Auditory images of those sounds that one has already heard. Standard questions: "What did I just say?" "Remember the melody of your favorite song."

Ak (right side view) - audio design. Images of those sounds that people have never heard before. Standard questions: "Imagine the noise of applause against the background of singing birds," "How would your name sound if you said the opposite?".

A (look down left) - closed audio performances. Conversation with yourself, internal conversation. Standard questions: "Say something you usually say to yourself," "Repeat a passage from each text next to you."

K (right view) - kinesthetic images of any type. Emotional as well as tactile, muscular, etc. feeling. Standard questions: "How do you feel when you touch a pinecone?" "How do you feel when you run?"

Another case is possible when the view of the interlocutor is directed straight ahead. This most often means that some external visual images pass before his eyes, and he not only participates in the conversation but, to some extent, is influenced by them. The criterion is a change in the eyes' focus to "examine" imaginary objects and a slightly missing facial expression.

Also, note that observing the internal process of finding an answer to a question from the person you are talking to, you will notice not one but several consecutive views. The reason is the three-stage process of reflection, which is common to all people.

In the first stage—extracting the necessary information—one must gain access to his memory. This is done with the help of the "key"—visual image, sound, or bodily sensation. The presentation system (visual, auditory, or kinesthetic) used to "open" memory is called a presenter and reveals significant differences between people. NLP even introduces the terms "visualize", "kinesthetic," "audio"—according to the leading system specific to a person. If, say, the word "cat" is uttered, then Visualize will visualize it, Audialist may hear a meow first, and Kinesthetics will most likely recall the feeling of caressing soft hair.

In the second stage, the information extracted from the memory must be brought to consciousness. Here it will also be presented in the form of visual, sound, or kinesthetic images. The specific person used for this purpose by representations is called representative (representing). Each of us again has our favorite representation system (one of the three possible), with the help of which we are more accustomed to keep in mind the necessary information and work with them.

The last, third stage is to check the integrity of the information received. And this is aided by the inherent inner sensations of each individual of the same three types as if signaling the right or wrong solution to the problem. You've probably often heard phrases: "I feel something is wrong here!" Or "I see I'm wrong," etc., which unknowingly shows your criterion for a hidden test. The corresponding system of representations in NLP is called a reference (verification).

So, remember the three stages of thought when looking for the answer to the question:

1. The master system provides access to information stored in memory using images of one of three types (visual, sound, kinesthetic).
2. Representative system presents information to the consciousness, ensures its introduction and work with it in one form or another.
3. The reference system verifies the truth of the information and gives a signal for evaluation —also in the form of images of a certain type.

Here is a specific example of the analysis of the work of the line of sight consciousness. You asked someone you know to remember the color of his father's eyes and to observe, say, such a sequence of reactions. First, the gaze goes left up (zone Bb), then right down (zone K), and finally left down (zone A).

It can be assumed that the partner first saw his father in the imagination, then experienced the kinesthetic sensations he experienced in his presence, and finally orally commented on the result. Only after going through such a sequence (called strategy in NLP) will you hear the answer. To make sure the assumption is correct, ask the other person if this was the case. Most people are not used to following their internal strategies, but they are fully capable of implementing them.

You can find out in which system of representations a person's consciousness is currently working on learning how to analyze the oculomotor reactions of the interlocutor quickly.

The additional signs will allow you to understand how a person emotionally relates to his inner images, how important they are to him. There are many such secondary signs, although they are no longer so unambiguous. For example, in an irritated state in some people, the iris of the eyes darkens, while in others, the same thing happens at the moment of great joy. Facial pallor also has several "decipherments." It is even more difficult to interpret the changes in posture, micromotion of the arms, the tension of the facial muscles, etc.

Nevertheless, Dr. Bandler strongly recommends that you strive to notice and make sense of as many signs as possible.

In the first stage of such training, it is better to ask questions to good friends, from which you can without hesitation indicate the results of observation. Noticing any new sign or reaction whose meaning is not yet clear to you, try to understand what they are feeling at the moment, in what condition they are.

As you acquire certain skills, start working with strangers, comparing questions to the situation, or just watching someone else's conversation. So, you can even train in transport on the way to work. Your goal at this stage is to learn how to move entirely to the analysis of the interlocutor. In NLP, this state is called actual time. In it, you completely forget about yourself and live only in the flow of information coming from the outside world. All inner feelings and sensations should be discarded as interference, or, rather, descending into the subconscious. Then the consciousness is released, and you can fully focus on the other person.

Here are some more sample questions that encourage the interlocutor to look for the non-verbal answers you need, that is, to create different imaginations.

Searching for images in memory (one sees the situation from the inside):

- Centuries "How many buttons are on your favorite jacket?"

- AB - Remember the sound of the surf.
- Ap - Imagine the feeling of a jet of water in the shower.

Look for images that are not in memory and need to be "constructed" (one sees the situation from the outside):

- Bk - Imagine your boss as an angel.
- Ak "How does a door creak in a Viking dugout?"
- k.k. - How would you feel when you parachute?

Training with such questions is best done by three people. One person seeks an answer but does not utter it immediately in words. Another, noting the direction of the respondent's gaze, makes assumptions about those images that have been replaced in his mind, and tries to talk about them as fully as possible (using additional characters). For example, if a person is asked to remember how he drove a car, then with a visual representation of the movement of his eyes, they can resemble the gaze of a fast-moving car. With a kinesthetic, you will notice the legs' involuntary movement, as if pressing the accelerator.

If the issue does not cause severe oculomotor reactions, it is necessary to complicate it. Then the respondent will be completely busy looking for the answer, and his reactions will become more natural.

The third participant complements the analysis of the second with his comments (another life experience will help achieve greater completeness of the result and will also create a useful atmosphere of the competition).

Then the partners change roles until each of them visits all three. The described exercise perfectly develops the first skills for observation of the interlocutor, without which it is impossible to become a master of interpersonal communication.

Eyes - a universal lie detector

The eyes are one of the most modern lie detectors. Through the movement of the eyeballs, you can determine what a person is thinking at the moment, whether he is telling the truth or lying. People move their gaze in certain directions, depending on the type of thinking. Eye observation is one of the simplest methods of obtaining information about a person's thoughts and emotions.

Studies show that the pupil expands completely by 45% if we like what we see and conversely narrows if we do not like it. It always happens that a human narrows his eyes when he or she feels unpleasant emotions. Such eye reactions last about 1/8 of a second, but you'll catch them if you look closely. One possibility for non-verbal cues involving the eyes is eye blockage. If a human, in reaction to visual or auditory input, covers his or her eyes with his or her hand, brushes his or her eyelid, or simply closes his or her eyes for a split second, it reveals negative emotions from the information received. Such a reaction can even provoke your thoughts. It is worth noting that during stress, the movement of the eyes is recognized. When a person experiences positive emotion, the eyes will be wide open, eyebrows raised. Also, the widening of the eyes is observed in a moment of surprise.

Decrypt eye movement

- The movement of the eyes to the left

(Image memory). If we imagine things from our experience: "What color is your car?" then, along with the verbal response, you'll get a left-hand feel, characteristic of visual memories.

"When was the last time you ever saw this guy?"

- Defocusing the eyes

The eyes are out of focus, and their position is fixed, the pupil is slightly dilated. Visual images can be from memory or projected.

- The movement of the eyes up to the right

The constructed image. Visual representation of images, events, or objects that we haven't seen before, or representation of events and objects that we haven't seen before. "What's that cow going to look like?"

We have heard the auditory recollection of those sounds before. "How does your favorite song sound?"

Hearing construction. The auditory representation of sounds that we have never before heard. "How does your dream song sound?" "How would your phone sound, if you had your hand covering it?"

- Movement of the eyes down to the left

Internal conversation. The direction of the eyes matches the role of speech control when a person chooses the words he wants to pronounce. The interpreter can often see this view during the interpretation by the student regarding the defense of the diploma by the interviewer.

- Eyes down to the right

The sensation of emotions, tactile sensations, sensation of movement, smell. "How do you feel when you're upset?" "When you play games, how do you feel?" "Do you remember how to bake a burn?" The important point is that it is impossible to construct sensations—we cannot imagine those feelings that we have not experienced.

There is a typical pattern of eyeball movement called the "Lie Detector": the direction of gaze from the visual structure (right up, right horizontal) to speech control (left down); in the inner experience it corresponds to such a sequence - First visualize, create how it might be, and then just state what it refers to, nothing more.

And now a few examples from life.

During an interrogation, the investigator asked the woman: What relations did you have with the citizen "K"?

Answer: "We were friends." — and lowers her eyes to the right down. It enters kinesthetics (sensory memories). Judging by the response of the brain, including the recollection of the senses, we can infer that the woman was telling a lie.

Similar situation: The spouse comes back from a get-away, the wife asks: "How could you bite the dust?" The spouse answers: "It was exhausting," and he brought down his eyes to one side. It goes into sensations (tactile recollections). It is too soon to finish up the falsehoods, yet we can say that he has something to recall.

Question: What happened at your gathering

Answer: "Not all that much, we talked and bid farewell." The eyes go left - up, while the pupils slender. The recollections evoked negative feelings. It tends to be expected that a squabble emerged at the gathering.

The gaze controls the course of the conversation, regulates the activity and distance of the interlocutors. The eyes help keep in touch when you speak. People look at each other from 1/3 to 2/3 of the talk time. The speaker usually looks less at the partner than at the listener. This allows him to concentrate more on the content of his speeches without being distracted. But at the end of his speech, the speaker usually looks directly into the listener's face, as if signaling the end of his speech. The one who takes the floor usually looks away first and then starts talking. If the interlocutors are seen too often, then perhaps they are more interested in the interlocutor than in what he says. If a person meets the gaze of a conversation partner for less than 1/3 of the communication time, then they accept it.

From the point of view, people are often in a hurry to make judgments about a person: for example, if a person's gaze is direct and open, then the person himself is such and if he "hides his eyes"—most likely insincere, unfriendly. Such a conclusion may be hasty. Some people do not want to be seen, that is, to be in the spotlight, which is why they "hide their eyes" in conversation. Others like to attract the attention of others, which may be the reason for their direct gaze, not for the openness of the character. Studies show that if interlocutors sit on opposite sides of a wide table, they look at each other more often than when they sit at a narrow table. In this way, the increase in the distance between the partners is compensated by increasing the frequency of viewings. The emotions experienced during the conversation also affect the appearance: positive emotions are accompanied by an increase in the number of views when discussing a pleasant topic. It is easy to look into the interlocutor's eyes. Negative feelings are characterized by a refusal to look at the interlocutor—we avoid doing this if it is something less pleasant.

The eyes can make different movements during a conversation. It is useful to be able to read these signals more effectively with people. Here are examples of such movements. Moving the eyes down (lowering the eyes) shows that a person is very worried about what others are saying. Eyes facing up and to the left mean that the listener is completely absorbed in the content of the speech. Eyes pointing up and to the right show that the listener is characterized by great care and experience to compare what is said with their own experience and knowledge.

A person's self-esteem and status affect how often people look at each other in the process of communication. You can observe two glances at the same time— "bottom-up" and "top-down." The first look "bottom-up"—the head is bent, and the eyes seem to be forced to look up. It can be seen when a person wants to help, to emphasize his attention, humility. Also, such a view is found in secretive people: aggressive and cautious (they still have stressed movements throughout the body). This view is often seen in anxious, restless people, modest and shy, conscientious, and executive.

If a person during a conversation looks down, as if he is trying for some reason to remove another from the field of view, perhaps he is unpleasant or uninteresting to him. Noticing this look from your interlocutor, you should keep in mind: something causes a negative reaction, and you need to change something, unless, of course, the partners are interested in successful interaction. But sometimes people in conversation close their eyes for a short time because they agree and approve of the words of a communication partner. Thus, the same sign, considered outside the context of communication, can be incorrectly assessed.

If the interlocutor looks at him for a long time, a stare ("glazed") look, this probably means that he misses half of what was said. Maybe something is pressing him, it is not easy for him, most likely at the moment when he does not have the situation under control.

When the interlocutor listens sincerely, he can unconsciously turn his eyes, this lively restless look—a sign that he is making an effort to understand the meaning of the words fully, is interested in conversation, or waiting for an important discussion. But if the rotating movements are too fast, this may be a signal of his uncertainty.

Business view: Focused on a triangle formed by a combination of three points—the eyes and the middle. If you look at this triangle most of the time during a business contact, you can create a serious, business-like conversation. This view is also called direct, accompanied by openness, and willingness to communicate, the truthfulness of statements, and free discussion of acute problems. A variety of business views can be attributed to a flattened, centered view. When the students of the discussion partners move from the centers to each other and freeze in this position, the partners seem to see a problem in front of them. Such an opinion arises when discussing a specific, complex, and urgent situation.

Social ("secular") look: Best suited for neutral communication. The gaze of one of the communicators falls below the level of the other's eyes towards him and falls into the eye-mouth triangle.

An intimate gaze occurs when the gaze is shifted downward to other parts of the interlocutor's body. The interlocutors seem to be looking at each other, often without noticing it themselves.

Side view: You can see when the pupils of the eyes are moving right or left at the same time. So they look left or right when the person does not trust the interlocutor, they are critical, negative about a person or information.

If the eyes are narrowed, then mistrust is accompanied by aggressive emotions, and if it is open, then the person wants to hide the fear. Often appears in a person who is used to control the situation, to manage it. He carefully observes everything that happens around. Less often, squatting is a message of interest.

Most often, the side blink carries information about contempt for whom it is necessary to communicate it to, for a great reluctance to reveal itself even in the smallest.

Avoiding gaze: Thrown by people out of fear, timidity. And it is also found in those who want to deceive others. This gaze is unpleasant—it is constantly moving from the face, from the hands to the clothes, then to the other parts of the body and again to the face. You never know what this person thinks, even if he agrees with you, he has no faith. Among the deceptive views can be distinguished the thief's gaze (fleeting escapes from the opposite gaze) and the deceiver's stare (eyes that run fast in all directions, eyebrows in the form of thin ropes).

Evaluate the appearance or look at a meeting: So ("from head to toe") only a person who is confident in the situation and can control it, explores another.

A lethargic look: Can be seen in very calm, non-emotional people or any person in a boring, or familiar situation. You may be left with the impression that a person is asleep. This may be the gaze of a lazy, short-sighted person, whose facial features are bulging and has watery eyes, with a gaze that moves slowly from object to object.

Aggressively insulting: Demonstrated by those who like to show their clear superiority, strength, ready to "crush" the other. On such a person—there is contempt or emptiness, no emotions, and the interlocutor is not visible.

Piercing look: It is often found among those who have the authority, and the duty to demand laws, work, reports, instructions, and, also, have the right to accuse.

A controlling gaze: Characteristic of observant people who follow even the smallest actions, movements, and words of others.

Oily look: This is a palpable, unceremonious, hidden look. A wink often accompanies it. A variety of this appearance can be considered the look of a careless person, but the eyelids are blue.

An enchanted species: Can be seen in a person in an elevated state, captivated by the strongest emotional experiences close to ecstasy.

Access is the process of receiving inside information from the interlocutor—photos, sounds, words, sensations that build memories, fantasies, etc.

You can determine your partner's experience, his or her dominant representation system, and his or her type of thinking using "access keys."

Access keys are specific non-verbal behavior that show how information is obtained.

The information you need for human representative

systems can be obtained in many different ways and observing eye movement is the easiest.

The access keys are eye movements

The "scanning" models of oculomotor reactions are related to the internal processes needed to update the mind about memories or to build future experiences.

You can be sure that the person is gaining internal access to the corresponding representative system when you catch any of the oculomotor reactions. You can determine which representative systems they are using if you observe the eye movement of a communication partner.

The hypnologist observes the movements of the partner's eyes and uses key predicates that correspond to the position of the client's eyes. Not only that. The direction of the gaze can tell you whether he is remembering something stored in his memory, some experience that happened in the past or building something new for himself.

People systematically move their eyes in certain directions, depending on what type of thinking is found in them. Eye movements are often combined with purely individual reactions, taking into account the person's actual attitude to the mental images that appeared in front of him (eyes went to the left and pupils narrowed—an unpleasant auditory memory of something).

We will now present the eye movements again that provide the most important information in nonverbal communication. The direction of the gaze is indicated by the object you are observing. If it's "left," it means to his left hand, not yours. Well, and to the right, respectively. You are unlikely to confuse the top and bottom.

1. - The Movement of The Eyes to The Left

Eidetic image (image-memory). When we see it from our experience: "What color is the wallpaper in your room?" And together with the verbal response, you will get a left look, typical of visual memories.

"What color was your friend's suit yesterday?"

2. - Defocusing the eyes

The eyes are out of focus, and their position is fixed, the pupil is slightly dilated. Visual images can be eidetic or projected.

3. - The Movement of The Eyes Up to The Right

The constructed image. Virtual representation of images, events, or objects that we haven't seen before. "What will an orange elephant look like in raspberry spots?"

The auditory recollection of those sounds we have heard before. "How does your phone alarm sound?"

Hearing construction. The auditory representation of sounds we have never heard before. "What does your name sound like if you say the opposite?" "How will your alarm clock ring if you cover it with a metal bucket?"

4. - "Phone position" eye movement down to the left

Internal dialogue closed the auditory presentation.

Conversation with yourself, internal conversation. This point of view coincides with the function of speech control when one carefully chooses the words to be uttered. This view can often be seen with the interpreter during the interpretation, with the reporter making a responsible report with the interviewer.

5. - Eyes down to the right

Kinesthetic presentation. The sensation of emotions, tactile sensations, sensation of movement, smell. How do you feel when you feel joy? What do you feel when you run? "Do you remember how mustard plaster burns?" Interestingly, there are no constructions in kinesthetic—we cannot imagine those sensations that we have not experienced.

How to understand the interlocutor for eye movement

The eyeballs move according to what sensory process is currently going on in mind. In most cases, this movement serves as a fairly reliable indicator of how a person's mind works.

There is even a typical pattern of eyeball movements called a "lie detector": the direction of gaze from the visual structure (right up, right horizontal) to speech control (left down); in the inner experience it corresponds to such a sequence—first imagine, construct how it could be and then say only what corresponds to it, nothing more.

"I believe! These eyes do not lie. After all, how many times has he said it?"

If this is your belief, then this is your main mistake. You underestimate the value of human eyes.

Understand that language can hide the truth, and eyes sometimes cannot see!

Suppose you are asked a sudden question, you don't even flinch, and in one second you take control of yourself and know what you need to tell to hide the truth. You say it very convincingly and not a single fold of your face moves, but, alas, worried by the question, the truth from the bottom of the soul for a moment jumps in the eyes, and it's over. It's been spotted, and you're caught!

I don't know what a husband who is also a father is like, but he will be the best lover if he goes on an inner-kinesthetic experience. His inner experience is connected with kinesthetic—with touches, caresses....

The upward movement of the eyeballs occurs with a predominance of visual processes, and the side, with a predominance of auditory. Looking down is usually associated with kinesthetic sensations or internal dialogue.

The nature of eyeball movements also depends on whether the invocation process is in progress or whether sound or visual images are recreated. For instance, when scrolling through possible scenarios related to something that has never happened to you before.

The pattern of eyeball movement is called the "lie detector"—for example, the direction of gaze from the visual or auditory structure to the control of speech—this in the internal experience corresponds to this sequence.

So, the upper floor is visual, and the middle floor is auditory, the lower is divided between kinesthetics and speech control. It is convenient to use the property on the left to facilitate orientation, which is "more true" than the right.

The oculomotor response patterns have a reasonable neurophysiological rationale. Eye movement up and to the left is the usual way people use to stimulate the dominant hemisphere as a method of accessing visual memory.

The upward movement of the eyes to the right, on the contrary, stimulates the left hemisphere of the brain and gives constructive images. That is, a visual representation of things that one has not seen before.

You can check by asking yourself simple questions.

Ask your partner questions that will trigger memory images, for example:

- What color is the front door of your apartment?
- What does your bedroom look like?

Examples of audio questions:

- Do you remember the song you liked?

Or kinesthetically:

- How do you feel when you dive into the sea?
- How do you feel that you are hungry?

Lack of attention to the access keys often confuses. You often hear complaints:

"My son doesn't listen to me at all. We sit in the same room, I tell him something, and he pretends not to hear me. "

In this case, the dissatisfied mother was busy with her inner images and tried to get a sound response, but she did not notice what was happening "outside," to put it mildly. Namely, those moments when the son perceives the information as indicated by his eyes.

What does a gaze mean, the direction of the gaze, the dilated, and narrowed pupils? Careless acting looks, looking below, left, right, up, down, and blinking often? The look and the direction of the gaze can say a lot about a person's thoughts, feelings, and experiences.

Let's start with the pupils (Look into my eyes, and you will see the truth)

Pupils expand or contract under certain lighting. It all depends on the mood and brightness of the lighting. If a person is emotionally agitated, then his pupils become slightly dilated than in the same light, at rest. The same thing happens when a person looks at something he likes. They don't just say, "my eyes are on fire." A person with dilated pupils looks the most attractive and enchanting. But if the pupils narrow, then aggression, anger, and irritation increase in a person.

Raised eyebrows (sign, gesture- Hey, hello!)

Eyebrows are raised when we notice a pleasant person next to us, and we want him to notice us. This is nothing more than an expression of interest. People who stay with a stony face and do not raise eyebrows when greeting are considered aggressive, sympathy for them is much less. Know that if you raise your eyebrows, the person will certainly repeat your gesture and maybe even smile back.

Raised eyebrows in women (Gesture, sign - Hold me or obey)

Women with raised eyebrows and large eyes are considered submissive, which is why they are very successful with men. Men want to hug and defend. In men, everything is different; the lower the eyebrows, the narrower the eyes. So, men want to show their authority and seriousness. Recently, however, women have begun to use this view. And if the eyebrows are thick, then they are as aggressive as powerful and able to conquer.

Looking below (Gesture, sign - playing with you)

If a woman's head is slightly tilted and looking down, it is a signal of humility, which men like so much. It gives the woman a look of "childish naivety and purity of soul." Such a look evokes real parental feelings. And if a smile complements all this, then the effect is simply stunning. In a dispute, the interlocutor is likely to take the side of the person who looks cute and obedient from below.

The scenario can be viewed from two sides. If it is

complemented by a flirtatious smile and a sparkle in your eyes, then you are interested in the interlocutor. Women use this "hated" look during flirting. But if in addition to the look on his face there is a smile with lowered corners of the lips and frowning eyebrows, then the interlocutor is most likely hostile, and it is better to hide from his field of vision.

Frequent blinking (gesture, sign - stick with eyes)

Usually, a person blinks about 10-20 times a minute. Did your interlocutor start blinking harder? Only in this way, often blinking, his brain wants to "throw" your image from the subconscious. When a person starts blinking stubbornly, closing his eyes for 2-3 seconds, you should know that he is just tired of communicating with you and cannot tell you about it personally due to embarrassment or other reasons. In this case, it is better to find another person to talk to and continue to communicate with.

Running eyes (Gesture, sign, look - Where is the way out...)

Did you notice that your interlocutor's eyes began to flow from one side to the other? No, no! He is not doing gymnastics for the eyes! He is looking for a way to withdraw (or looking for a target if he is a special intelligence agent). He is tired of your conversations, or they are not interesting to him. He might even try to smile with pursed lips in return, imitating interest, but you know, most likely when you turn your back, he will run away.

Social look (See, gesture, sign - Just talking through the eyes)

During normal communication, the interlocutor's eyes "draw" a triangular area that affects the eyes and nose. In this area, we focus on a simple situation that is safe for us. Such a view is not considered aggressive or hostile. This is how communication between people of the same status and age takes place. Easy and simple.

Intimate look (Intimate "conversation" through the eyes)

Thanks to improved peripheral vision, women can discreetly examine a man, keeping their eyes everywhere. But men do not know how to do this, and they carefully examine the object of their adoration. The intimate gaze "outlines" a triangle between the eyes and its tip forms on the chest, and if people are at a distance, it passes from the eyes down to the inguinal area. The look is not hostile, meaning that the person most likely wants something more than communication with you.

Authoritative look (authoritative conversation with eyes)

The authoritative gaze is centered in the triangle between man's eyes and "his mythological third eye" above the eyes along the bridge of the nose. Usually, this view is used by authoritative, confident people. It carries the strength and desire to suppress the interlocutor. People with a mild temper are sometimes advised to use this look to look more serious, complementing it with lowered eyebrows and narrowed eyes. It is with this look that the interlocutor can interrupt an annoying conversation.

He looks up-down, right-left

Where do the eyes of the man sitting opposite look? The eyes are the mirror of the soul! If the eyes are directed up to the left, then the person is most likely trying to remember the image he has seen before or what he has done before. And if down to the right, then we recall the emotions and feelings with which this or that action was performed. If it is directed from the left to the ear, the person remembers the melody or the sound heard, and if he mysteriously looks down to the left, an internal dialogue takes place. Such views do not last long and pass almost instantly, and the main thing is to catch them.

Head straight, head up

The raised head is typical of people who participate in a conversation. This position is neutral, does not bring aggression, or, on the contrary, deep indifference. Small nods can supplement a raised head during a conversation, or a person can rub his chin, thinking about what has been said or heard. In any case, you can be sure that the interlocutor is listening to you (unless he froze with an unblinking look, most likely in a trance in this situation). If the chin is forward and slightly upwards and is accompanied by a kind of downward gaze, then the person is arrogant, and you need to be more careful when talking to him.

Tilt head to the side—a look with a tilt of the head

A sloping head on one side is a symbol of humility. At this point, the person wants to show; he does not pose a threat because he opens his throat. Also, tilting one side shows interest in the conversation. Often, to look more attractive, women bow their heads in the presence of a man. By often showing people a "defenseless" neck, you can bring them closer to you.

The head is lowered forward (Sign of disapproval, the gesture of aggression)

Bulls always set their horns forward when they are aggressive. A bowed head and a look of gloom with eyebrows and dilated nostrils gather signals for others about a person's negative and aggressive mood. That he is ready to tear to pieces anyone who will not be favorable to him or will not be pleasant to him. So, you better wait until one straightens one's head or at least tilts it to the side. Otherwise, each of your words may have the effect of a "red rag," and you may be "lifted by the horns."

All the above gestures, points of view, and examples can only be used in context and are not an exact indication of one or another decipherment of actions. Remember that you should not judge by just one criterion and interpret actions in your direction. Don't be biased.

CHAPTER 9

BODY LANGUAGE MISTAKES TO AVOID

An old saying goes that a photo is worth a thousand words.

But how much is body language worth?

During a conversation, the words that come out of your mouth are far from the only form of communication.

We all have ways and a posture when speaking that say a lot about what we are feeling at each moment.

Some of them are universal and even easy to understand.

Of course, you need to know what to look for and have mastery over each gesture's meanings.

A simple change of voice, for example, can indicate fear, irritation, or even that the person in front of you is about to cry.

This goes for both personal and professional levels.

Do you want to find out what some of these actions, which are usually involuntary, mean?

Body language and its reading are not an exact science. There are no hard and fast rules for interpreting unspoken signals. Even scientists trained to read people like a book make mistakes, especially when observing experienced players who consciously control their behavior.

Positive Body Language

Positive body language includes proper eye contact, active engagement/listening, and targeted gestures that emphasize the message you are trying to convey. Research shows that people who use positive body language are more confident, competent, and more convincing and have more emotional intelligence.

Here's how it works:

1. Positive body language changes your attitude

It has been discovered that consciously adjusting body language to make it more positive improves your attitude because it has a strong effect on your hormones.

2. Increases testosterone

If we think about testosterone, we typically concentrate on sports and rivalry, but testosterone's value covers much more than athletics. Whether you're a man or a woman, testosterone improves confidence in yourself and makes others see you as being more reliable and positive. Research indicates that positive body language raises 20 percent of the testosterone levels.

3. Reduces cortisol

Cortisol is a stress hormone that interferes with work and creates negative effects on health in the long run. Lowering cortisol levels minimizes stress and allows you to think more clearly, especially in difficult and challenging situations. Research shows that positive body language reduces cortisol levels by 25 percent.

4. It creates a powerful combination

Although a decrease in cortisol or an increase in testosterone is great in itself, the two are a powerful combination commonly seen in people in positions of power. This combination creates self-confidence and clarity of mind that are ideal for dealing with tight deadlines, difficult decisions, and large amounts of work. It is known that people who have naturally high testosterone levels and low cortisol levels manage to work under pressure.

5. Make yourself feel nicer

In a study by Tufts University, subjects viewed audio recordings of doctors communicating with their patients. Only by observing the doctors' body language could the respondents guess which doctors eventually sued their patients. Body language is a huge factor in your perception and can be more important than your voice or even what you say. Learning to use positive body language would make people respect you and have more trust in you.

6. Transfer jurisdiction

Researchers found, in a study carried out at Princeton, that one second of a candidate's footage for senator or governor was enough for people to predict exactly which candidate was elected. Although this does not improve your confidence in the voting process, it does demonstrate that there is a clear basis in body language for the interpretation of competence.

7. Improves your emotional intelligence

Your ability to effectively express your feelings and ideas is essential to your emotional intelligence. Individuals whose body language is negative have a contagious and damaging impact on those around them. Working to enhance your body language affects your emotional intelligence profoundly.

We often think of body language as a result of our attitude or how we feel. That is true, but psychologists have also shown that it is true and vice versa: a change in body language also changes your attitude.

Negative Body Language

Hands close to the mouth: Passing the hand over the lips, placing objects close to the mouth, and touching the chin can indicate the attempt to fail with the truth, as of someone afraid of being caught in the act.

Clenched lips: Compressed and closed lips can denote that you try to avoid saying what you think or not wanting to answer a question that has been asked. In the ride of this action, the closed jaw can also be an acute sign of stress and a message that there is discomfort in being in that situation.

Looking without direction: Looking is, without a doubt, one of the most expressive parts of our body, being possible to perceive when someone is sad or even very happy from it. In the analysis of body language, looking up or right usually indicates a certain confusion (like looking for a mental image while winding up). Upwards or without direction can denote irritation and contempt.

To contract the forehead is a sign seen with certain negativism because a certain doubt, tension and even nervousness can appear.

Crossed arms: This gesture may be one of the ones that most create physical barriers between the communicator and his receiver, and it may show certain irritability or rejection to the moment he is going through.

Body Language Mistakes to Avoid

Body language is one of the most important vehicles to interact with. During a conversation, speech or pitch, you always use facial expressions, body gestures, and hand movements to communicate your message.

Using facial expressions, body gestures, hand movements, and the body language of the legs, you can stream your content with success and show confidence.

If you use this inappropriately or inaccurately, they can become a source of distraction for your audience, and it can conflict with your message.

1. The different hand movements

A very common mistake of people in meetings, conversations, and presentations is certainly the language of the hands.

Hiding your hands, shaking them, or moving them too much demonstrates your nervousness and can give your audience the feeling that you don't believe what you're saying.

Keeping your hands in your pockets is also a gesture that indicates that you are afraid, not knowing where to go or not interested in what you are doing.

If that were not enough, it could still make your interlocutors think that you are unkind to them. Remember that if you don't look confident, people won't buy whatever you are saying.

Instead, try to keep your arms in front of you openly. Use your hands to explain your point of view through concise and calculated movements.

Watch your hand movements; this can testify against you.

2. Crossed arms

Crossing your arms can also give you the impression that you are enthusiastic about the information you are going to give, or something is wrong.

It is a defensive posture that will signal defense and resistance and create a distance between you and your audience.

Instead, keep your arms open and at a distance from your body, almost as if you are giving a big bear hug.

This open gesture is engaging and welcome. It will convey a message of peace and confidence to your audience.

3. Avoiding eye contact

Avoiding eye-to-eye contact with your audience and looking at your watch, your feet, or constantly looking at the presentation screen, will make you sound playful and unprofessional.

Instead, always consider making eye contact with your audience when expressing your ideas.

Moving your head quickly during the presentation will portray that you are personally interested and involved.

4. Bad posture

The position is one of the most important attributes of body language while delivering a presentation.

If you are leaning your back and shoulders in a posture that lets your neck hang, it will defiantly convey a weak message, and your audience can start thinking about your professionalism.

Instead, point in a neutral direction, regardless of whether you are sitting or standing.

Adopting a bad posture will make you feel bad.

5. Doing bad body movements

Walking back and forth by moving your arms quickly will give your posture a totally strange feeling.

Instead, if you need to move in any way in your meeting or presentation, that move must have a purpose. It is also important not to just stand in one place.

Interact with everyone during your presentation so that you can send a positive message to all parties.

6. Watch your legs

During a presentation, the legs are the most difficult members to control because of nervousness or concentration to convey the best ideas and a good image.

Constantly shaking your legs if you are standing will signal to your audience that you are uncomfortable and restless, which is not a good thing. They want to feel that you are giving yourself completely to the meeting.

Instead, make controlled movements for the audience.

When you move during a conversation or presentation, make the audience feel that you have been practicing these movements before—make them believe that you are an experienced expert.

7. Forget to smile

Your face is the most important aspect of creating a good impression. Unless you are breaking bad news, it is appropriate that you are smiling, even during a business meeting.

Start your presentation or greeting with a smile, and as a result, the audience will receive your message more willingly.

Try to keep your smile on during the presentation, particularly when you want to make people laugh. People will respond to a smile with another smile in return.

The interaction is the key to a remarkable presentation.

Always smile, it will make a great impression on people.

8. Inappropriate use of hand gestures

Hand in the pocket is a body language of neglect and disinterest.

On the other hand, moving your hands during your presentation supports each word with a more powerful meaning.

Whenever you want to make an important point, emphasize your words with hand gestures. Your audience will remember the fact or the information better when you anchor it with a specific gesture.

TEST: Does your boss have emotional intelligence at work?

Keep an eye on his body language and hands.

Try to avoid these bodily gestures to make a professional impression.

For a salesperson, giving the image of professionalism and confidence is much more than just saying the right thing at the right time.

You need to look trustworthy, successful, and you still need to show that you have the credibility to talk about what you do. Companies and people want to partner with successful salespeople and companies!

If you start to observe your behavior, you will see that, even unconsciously, you will end up making some faux pas.

Carefully observing your movements in the middle of a meeting, presentation, and even an informal conversation will make you identify and correct your gestures to make the best impression possible.

Start now and ensure that your image is the image of a great seller in the medium term.

These are eight fatal body language mistakes you should avoid: remember them even when you're alone.

As you have seen, body language is very important. So, pay attention to your facial expressions, leg positioning, posture, and gestures with people.

CHAPTER 10

THE ART OF PERSUASION

Persuasion is the art of convincing anyone of anything!

Yes, it is possible to convince others to do what you want as long as it is good for them.

It is not manipulation, and it is not a way to get other people to fulfill your desires, much less a way to take advantage.

If that is your view of persuasion and looking for a way to control others, this chapter is not for you!

However, if you aim to implement actions beneficial to all parties involved, you will learn how to convince others using the most effective techniques.

Scientists have been studying the reasons behind the SIM for more than 60 years, and one thing is a consensus: convincing someone to do something is not just a reflection of charisma, it is science.

Whether to sell, to capture emails, to ask for help from someone influential in the market, to know what persuasion is and how to use it can bring many points of advantage for you and others.

What is persuasion: The secret weapon to convince people

Persuasion is a communication strategy that uses logical,

rational, or symbolic resources to induce someone to accept an idea, an attitude, or action.

Persuasion is not used only in copies, landing pages, or during a sales argument.

It is present in the most diverse situations of our day-to-day activities, such as when we try to convince someone close to making a decision that we think is correct or even when negotiating a discount in a store.

You certainly already influence people around you without even realizing it, either with attitudes or arguments. What you will find here is just one way to enhance your persuasive potential further.

Whether to convince your boss that you deserve a raise, to ask a favor for someone influential in your niche market, or even to make more sales online, knowing what persuasion is and how to apply it can mean the difference between failure and success.

The number 1 rule to convince anyone about anything is as much as possible about the person you want to convince and meeting their biggest objections.

This rule is so important that you should write it down to never forget it. Without it, no technique to increase your persuasion will work.

The right time to start an argument

You can know all about the best words to persuade someone, what body language you need to adapt, and even know what the person wants to hear.

However, if you choose the wrong time to use all of this, there is no point in knowing what persuasion is, you will fail to convince even the most flexible people.

People are more easily persuaded to thank someone, as they feel in debt.

And if anyone wishes to thank you for everything you've done, it may be a perfect idea to add what you already know about convincing. And, of course, to make people thank you for something, you need to send first before you can care about getting it.

Don't use YOUR strengths

Do you consider yourself good at writing? Or do you know how to use the best examples to convince someone of something? Perhaps your strongest point is your charisma.

But do you want to convince someone? Then, don't use your strengths.

Use those of the person you want to persuade!

It sounds strange, but our abilities determine the way we think and act. And different people think differently.

To persuade someone, you need to speak "the person's language." It's no use talking in Portuguese with a Japanese who doesn't know the language, right?

Empathy. This is the key to success in persuading people.

So, put yourself in the hands of your audience, and consider if and what he or she would want to be persuaded of.

It's not what you say that is important, but how you say it.

What is the profile of the person you want to convince?

Empathy is a special ingredient that will lead you to convince people. But to generate empathy, it is necessary to observe and understand the difference between the most common profiles, which are as follows:

1. People who think together vs. individually: Those who like to think alone need more time to decide. And preferably at a time when they are alone. Therefore, an email with several arguments is a good weapon to achieve this profile. Those who like to make group decisions love brainstorming sessions, and this can be a good opportunity to discuss ideas and thus convince a group thinker.

2. Who likes to speak vs. who prefers to listen: This difference between profiles is easy to see. Those who like to listen can easily pay attention to what you are saying, while those who prefer to speak tend to lose concentration. To hold these people's attention, put it in focus every time you speak. Or choose writing, which works well. To encourage listeners to speak and provide important information, ask very specific questions to avoid generic responses.

How to increase our capacity for persuasion

As John Ruskin said, "He who has the truth in his heart must never fear that his tongue lacks the power of persuasion." Probably this is the best option. However, psychology has studied other theories that can be very useful in certain specific situations.

Before continuing, know that by persuasion, we mean the ability to seduce, convince, impress, or fascinate a person.

Some psychological theories to improve persuasion

The term "persuasion" may have had some negative connotations in recent years. We live in a world of global uncertainty and strong consumerism. We are continually bombarded with advertisements that appear to be convincing, whose motives are not necessarily as straightforward or simple as they should be, but far from belonging to worthy causes.

It is therefore important to make the difference between persuasion and manipulation. The latter lies in honesty, which exists in persuasion but not in manipulation; from a persuasive perspective, the other knows, since this is how it was presented to him, that we are trying to convince him of something. In contrast, from a manipulative perspective, this information tends to be concealed, hidden.

Persuasion is understood as the ability to influence another person honestly, which gives a great advantage to the people who developed it. This is why it is important to know some theories that are valid over time.

The amplification hypothesis

A firm mentality, conveyed with confidence, is very immune to convincing. However, it softens if it is expressed with uncertainty. In this case, arguments based on an emotional basis are very resistant to logic, and vice versa.

So, by carrying this hypothesis promulgated by Clarkson, Tbormala, and Rucker to practice, your possibilities of influence will increase if the attitudes that you project have the same meaning as those of the interlocutor. This is precisely what gives a name to the theory: if you want to persuade someone on a sport-related subject and you both support the same sports team, for example, the power of your arguments will then be amplified.

The manipulation theory

This theory handles four maxims to seduce a person; ensuring that the information is as complete as possible, ensuring the authenticity of this information, its relevance to the subject matter, and presenting it in such a way that it can be fully understood by the other.

This hypothesis, which might sound very poor, is very rational and fair. As Ruskin said, if you have the facts on your hand, you don't have to think about not being convincing. However, it is necessary to be well prepared and to have great knowledge of the subject, as well as to know how to explain them, to convince someone.

Nonetheless, it is difficult to defend yourself against such a strategy, especially if your interlocutor is skillful with words. It is necessary to observe his nonverbal language, which reflects contradictions between the assurance of his speech and what his gestures say. Having a little idea of the subject, I can point out what the most fragile part of his argument is.

The priming theory

This psychological method of persuasion is commonly used in advertisement. It is focused on the networks of interaction that we need to create in our minds. Indeed, when memory is activated, a concept or a feeling, in turn, allows the activation, for a limited time, of everything associated with this memory. For example, if you are told about the breakfasts of your childhood, it will be much easier afterward to make you buy milk.

The priming must be very subtle; thus, the person being stimulated is not aware of how he is influenced, even if he knows that he is in an influence brand since it is a publicity question. In another case, we would speak of manipulation.

The standard of reciprocity

This is a widely accepted social norm. It's as simple as giving something and waiting for something else in return. It is not a voluntary act but established and accepted by all.

Carrying out this standard can be as simple as saying thank you. Faced with the offer you make to him, you wait for your interlocutor to send you this courtesy, and reciprocity must be proportional to the type of service rendered.

The principle of scarcity

In a way, all human beings need to control their world. Having free will over what surrounds us is important. This is why when something is scarce, the desire to have it increases.

This psychological technique is also widely used in the advertising world; think of the famous slogans. So, if you consider yourself a victim of this practice, ask yourself if you need the rare good, feeling, or emotion that is offered to you.

All of these psychological theories of persuasion go beyond the mere theoretical field. They have been put into practice and demonstrated to be functional. You have likely used them at some point in your life without even being aware of them.

Method of dark persuasion

How vital is persuasion to a leader? Can success be achieved without the power of persuasion? Studying the world's most influential leaders in various fields shows that knowing how to persuade is a fundamental skill for them.

Belief is a characteristic that allows us to influence others. For this, it is necessary to understand how to listen, have charisma, and credibility.

1. Persuading is not manipulating. Manipulation is coercion by force for someone to do something that is not in their interest. Instead, persuasion is getting people to do things that are also in their interest.

2. Persuade persuasive people. Everyone can be persuaded at a specific time, but that does not mean that it is short-term. To convince, it is necessary to identify the people who are in the right moment to be persuaded and to focus our energy on them.

3. Opportunity. Persuasion depends on context and timing.

4. Interest in being persuaded. It is impossible to convince someone who is not interested in what you are saying. People spend most of their time thinking about money, love, and health, so to be persuasive, it is essential to know how to speak correctly on these issues to attract people's attention.

5. Reciprocity forces. When someone does something for you, you feel compelled to return it. Helping each other to survive is part of human DNA. If we have small gestures with others, then it is easier to ask them for things.

6. Persistence. The person who is willing to insist on a goal becomes more persuasive. The great leaders of history could sustain their efforts and messages to the masses for a long time. It is the example of Abraham Lincoln, who lost eight elections before becoming president of the United States, but who maintained his effort throughout.

7. Congratulate. Congratulations positively affect everyone, and good-feeling people are more likely to trust you. Honestly, congratulating people, even for simple things, is an excellent way to convince them.

8. Set expectations. Much of persuasion goes through the ability to manage the expectations of the other.

9. Don't take anything for granted. Always defend your value, not in fact that your interlocutor does not need what you offer.

10. Create scarcity. Everything that has value is usually scarce. The persuaded must be led to believe that the product we offer is uncommon, even if it is a service.

11. Create urgency. You have to be motivated to make the other person believe that they must act immediately. If he is willing to be persuaded now, we should not let him think about it, for he may not be so receptive in the future.

12. Lean on images. What we see is more powerful than what we hear. You have to perfect the first impression that is given.

13. Tell the truth. Sometimes the most effective way to persuade someone is by saying things that no one else is willing to say. Hard facts are pervasive.

14. Build a good relationship. You have to be open and take relationships to a field in which the interlocutor feels comfortable.

15. Flexibility. The most flexible person is the one in control. Children are convincing because they are willing to go through many stages to get what they want (cry, pout, beg, be charming...).

16. Transfer energy. Some people drain energy from others. Instead, persuasive people know how to transfer their energy to others to motivate them. There are many ways: eye contact, physical contact, laughter ... or merely knowing how to listen.

17. Communicate clearly. If a preteen is not able to understand what we want to explain, it is too complicated. You have to simplify things until highlighting only what is essential.

18. Be prepared. You have to know more about the other person than what the other person knows about you. It is the best way to gain an advantage and be able to carry out more effective persuasion.

19. Keep calm. No one is effective when they are 'on.' In the tensest situations, it is best to remain calm and not show emotions. In conflict situations, people turn to the person who controls their emotions.

20. Be moderate. People are not comfortable in conflict. Try to lower the tension level, be reasonable, and avoid an emotional place based on self-control.

21. Trust. If you believe in what you do, you will always be able to persuade others.

CHAPTER 11

NEURO-LINGUISTIC PROGRAMMING

What is NLP?

NLP, which stands for Neuro-linguistic programming, is a topic that is increasingly mentioned and intrigued by both business circles and those interested in personal growth and development. It can often be found in recent business and management literature and personal development books. Also, there are more and more lectures about different NLP techniques, as well as texts, videos, and audio materials on the Internet.

As a result, more and more people are coming into contact with NLP techniques. As with all the novelties that attract attention, and at the same time offer different ways of thinking, the mention of NLP provokes different reactions. Sometimes it can be heard that it is a matter of manipulating or selling fog, while some will even back down when they come in contact with an NLP expert, fearing the influence of that person. But what exactly is behind the word NLP?

How did NLP come about?

To make it easier to answer the question posed, it is good to go back to the past, to the 1970s, the period when the foundations of what NLP is today were laid. Richard Bandler and John Grinder, two curious enthusiasts, a student of psychology and mathematics and a professor of linguistics, shared an interest in understanding what makes top psychotherapists (of the time) so excellent at communicating and working with people.

They were interested in how they think, how they experience themselves, others, and the world around them in general, and what they specifically do to achieve results that no one else has achieved. Intensively and very systematically studying the work of three amazing people and experts, Fritz Pearls, Milton Erickson and Virginia Satir, they began to notice certain rules and patterns of their action. Which sometimes therapists themselves were not aware of, but did so intuitively, as a result of many years of reflection and experience.

Imitating experts

Understanding how those experts work, Bandler, and Grinder themselves began to apply this through contact with other people and realized that they could achieve similar results. For them, it was the beginning of discovering the path to excellence, which they decided to share with everyone else. Soon, their work began to be influenced by other top experts of the time. They studied human nature (such as Gregory Bateson, British anthropologist, linguist, and systems researcher), which resulted in the further development of NLP, which continues today.

NLP is still evolving

In its 40 years of existence, NLP and its many researchers

and creators have maintained a spirit of curiosity, and have continued to study the experiences of top practitioners in various fields of human activity, adding findings from the research and scientific milieu to contribute to a systematic study of human activity. Nature, but also (what is perhaps more important) ways to develop and make the best use of the opportunities we have as a human species.

In addition to psychotherapy, NLP is successfully used in leadership, business, sports, education, counseling, and other areas where there is interest in developing human resources and achieving excellence.

What is behind the (name) of NLP?

The very name Neuro-Linguistic Programming, coined by Bandler and Grinder to describe the knowledge they wanted to offer the world, conceals three key areas of NLP study:

Neuro - comes from the Greek word neuron (nerve cell) and refers to knowledge about the human brain and how we experience the world around us.

Linguistic - is the Greek word lingua (language) and refers to how our communication (both verbal and nonverbal) affects us and our environment.

Programming - refers to researching and understanding our "mental programs," i.e., the usual ways, habits, and strategies that we use in our actions, which sometimes help us, but also cause us to retaliate in achieving the desired goals and even leads us to unwanted results.

In the first step, NLP lets each individual know himself by getting to know how he experiences the world around him, communicating with him, and achieves (or not) his goals. In the next step, it offers an opportunity to get to know the ways of thinking and acting, which through human history and the successes of other great individuals (yes, NLP was fundamentally created by learning from success, not from mistakes) proved to be a good way to achieve quality communication. So, with others, all to solve the same life equation, the positive result of which we all strive for—a purposeful, fulfilled, and joyful life.

When you get a chance to get to know NLP better, the question you need to ask yourself is whether you are willing to learn how to live life to the fullest, achieve the desired results, and improve relationships with others.

If the answer is yes (you are ready for positive changes), then know that you are ready to allow all the knowledge and skills that NLP can offer you, bearing in mind that you are the one who will decide whether and how to use it in his life because the most important thing that NLP will always remind you of is that the person who has full responsibility for solving his life equation is just you.

Verbal vs. Non-Verbal Communication

To be a full member of society, communicate with other people, and achieve success, you must have communication tools, receive and transmit information, or communicate. The means of communication that a person uses are numerous and varied, but they can be combined into two groups: verbal and nonverbal.

Verbal communication and its role in human life

Verbal communication is considered to be an exclusively human form of communication. Its main means are words that have meaning and endowed with meaning, as well as messages that consist of words, such as texts or sentences.

Of course, animals also healthily exchange information. However, no matter how diverse, such communication is not speech, and the sounds emitted by animals do not signify objects or actions. They only convey a state, above all, emotionally.

Speech and language: communication and differences

Speech and language are very similar concepts, but they are not identical, although most people find it difficult to distinguish between speech and language. And here everything is very simple. Speech is a process of transmitting information, and language is how that process is carried out.

Language as a product of society

Language is social, and it is the result of long-term development, it originated and formed in society and is closely connected with a certain social environment. There are national languages that originated in the distant past. They have gathered a wealth of information about the history, culture, economy of an ethnos, mentality, way of life, and even its geographical location throughout millennial history. For example, in the Sami language—northern people living in Norway and Finland—there are more than 100 words for snow and ice, and in the Eskimo language, there are at least 500. In Kyrgyzstan, more than ten different words are used for names of different age groups of horses.

There are so-called Sub-languages: slang and dialects. They are formed in separate territorial or socio-professional communities based on the whole country. If dialects are no longer clearly expressed, then slangs are sometimes very strange in their sound and word meaning. These include youth slang, student slang, car enthusiasts, players, IT professionals, copywriters, etc.

Language is standardized both in terms of pronunciation and in terms of word order in a sentence. The rules of grammar and vocabulary are unshakable and must be followed by all native speakers; otherwise, they risk being misunderstood.

Every word has a meaning, that is, a connection with an object, phenomenon, or action. Remember, in S. Maršak's fairy tale "Cat's House," the cat explained to her guests: "This is a chair - they sit on it. This is a table - they eat on it." That is, she expressed the meaning of the terms. True, many words are polysemantic (semantics is the science of meaning). So, the word "chair" can mean more than just a piece of furniture. The words "key," "pencil," "mouse," etc. have several meanings.

In addition to meaning, a word has a different meaning, which is often individual. For example, the word "beauty" is not always praised, and it can have a meaning that is directly opposite to the meaning. Even more different meanings in holistic statements, which often leads to problems in understanding people who seem to speak the same language.

Speech and its features

If the language is social, then it is individual; it reflects the speaker's personality traits: education, social affiliation, temperament, the sphere of interest, emotional state, etc. The speech characteristics of a person enable him to create a full-fledged psychological portrait.

Their speech is filled with emotion. And the words we choose, the construction of sentences, and individual meanings depend on them. And it is closely related to non-verbal means such as intonation, volume, and tone of voice.

Speech functions

Speech can be considered an activity related to human interaction. Because this interaction is diverse, it then performs several functions:

- **Communicative** - a function of transmitting information, which is considered the main one.
  It is expressed in the transmission of emotions.
- **Motivation** - influencing other people to

encourage them to take any action or prohibition.

- **Significant** - the function of marking, manifested in the naming of objects, phenomena, and actions. The presence of this function is significantly different from the sound communication of animals.

Speech communication has a very high value in human communities, so it is so important that a child masters speech over time. And so, for a time, the mute was considered inferior and mentally retarded. However, as psychologists and linguists have discovered, with the help of verbal means in live interpersonal communication, people do not transmit more than 20% of the information. Is it amazing? But that is the case, 80% comes from nonverbal communication.

Nonverbal means and their types

When it comes to non-verbal means of communication, they primarily resemble gestures. However, gestures are relatively small, and the "youngest" group of non-speech means. Many of them are inherited from animal ancestors and are reflexive, so a person cannot control them.

Expressive reflex reactions

Such reflex reactions include expressive movements — external manifestations of those changes in the human body that accompany various emotional states. The most well-known and most noticeable expressive movements include the following:

- Redness and blanching of the skin, accompanying feelings of fear, anger or discomfort.
- Tremor - trembling of arms and legs, sometimes lips and vocal cords (fear, strong excitement).
- "Goosebumps" - a feeling associated with the excitation of hair follicles on the body (fear, excitement).
- Change in pupil size: dilatation - anxiety associated with a rush of adrenaline (fear, anger, impatience) and contractions (hostility, contempt, repulsion).
- Galvanic skin reaction (increased sweating) is accompanied by strong excitement, anxiety, often fear.

Because these nonverbal modes are based on natural reflex reactions that a person cannot control, these means of communication are considered to be the most sincere. A simple observation will help you identify the mismatch between a person's words and the feelings he is experiencing.

Olfactory communication tools

The oldest sources of information related to the human condition are olfactory means of communication. These are scents, primarily a person's natural scent. We have lost the ability of animals to be guided by smells, but they still influence the formation of attitudes towards other people, although we often do not notice this. The smell of sweat is traditionally thought to be unpleasant, but this is not always true. For example, the sweat of a person who is in a state of sexual arousal is saturated with pheromones, and its smell can be very appealing to a member of the opposite sex.

In addition to natural, artificial scents that create mood, excite, or relax, there is a certain value in communication. But the role of odorous agents in communication is perhaps the least studied.

Facial expressions and pantomimes

All the emotions and feelings we experience are reflected in our behavior and the nature of the movement. Just remember how a person's movement changes depending on his mood:

- With a smooth gait, a calm person walks slowly. And someone who confidently experiences a wave of strength, activity, and positive moves, walks widely and gives the green light as he walks. Also, his shoulders are turned—these are the movements of a successful, purposeful person.
- But if the mood is bad and the emotional state is depressed, then we see the gait becoming lethargic, stirring, the arms hanging down next to the body, and the shoulders drooping. Frightened people try to shrink, seem smaller, as if hiding from the world, pulling their heads into their shoulders and trying to make minimal movements.

In addition to dynamic pantomime means, there are also static ones. The position that a person occupies during a conversation can say a lot not only about his mood but also about his relationship with his partner, about the topic of conversation, about the situation as a whole.

Human movements are so informative that there is a whole direction in social psychology that studies body language, and many books are dedicated to it. Pantomime largely depends on the physiological state of the body, the change affected by emotions. Still, these are not reflex movements, and an educated person can learn to control them, show confidence in his absence, or hide fear. It is taught to politicians, actors, business people, and people of other professions, where it is important to influence people. In this sense, nonverbal communication is more effective because people believe words less than movements and gestures.

Even more diverse shades of emotions can be expressed on a person's face because of about 60 facial muscles. They can convey the most complex and clearest emotional states. Expressions can be joyful, upset, scared, cautious, contemptuous, repulsive, arrogant, timid, and so on. It is impossible to enumerate, let alone describe, different facial expressions.

However, as a rule, a person correctly guesses the meaning of mimic movements and can be seriously offended by the partner, even if he did not say anything offensive, but his appearance was eloquent. And children learn to "read" facial expressions from early childhood. I think a lot of people have noticed how a baby starts to cry when they see a mother frowning and blooming in a smile in response to her smile.

A smile is generally unique, standing out among nonverbal means of communication. On the one hand, a smile belongs to innate reflex reactions, many more animals, especially social ones, can laugh: dogs, dolphins, horses. On the other hand, this mimic reaction is highly valued as a means of communication that people have learned to control and even put into service. However, a careful person will still distinguish a sincere smile from a false demonstration of a tooth without caries.

Gesture

These are the most conscious and controlled nonverbal means. They are fully socialized and can even perform the functions of characters. The simplest example of such signs are numbers displayed with fingers. But many other gestures indicate prohibition, invitation, gestures of consent, denial, command, obedience, and so on.

The peculiarity of gestures is that they, like the words of a formal language, belong to a particular society or ethnos. So, they often talk about sign language. Different peoples may have the same sign for different gestures. And the same gesture often has a completely different meaning.

For example, the thumb and forefinger, connected in a ring, in a tradition that came to Europe from the United States, means "okay"—everything is fine. In both Germany and France, this same gesture has an almost opposite meaning—"zero," "empty," "nonsense,"; in Italy, it is "beautiful," "big," and in Japan "money." In some countries, such as Portugal and South Africa, such a gesture is generally considered rude, and in Tunisia and Syria, it poses a threat.

Thus, for normal understanding, it is necessary to study not only the language of the words of another nation but also sign language so as not to get into a mess accidentally.

Nonverbal agents associated with speech

Among the means of communication are those that do not play an independent role and are closely related to speech activity. But they are also called non-verbal means. It is the intonation with which pronunciation is pronounced, raising and lowering the tone, pause, volume, and speed of speech. Such tools also convey information about a person's emotional state. For example, the more excited and upset a person is, the faster and louder his speech becomes, and an indecisive voice and frequent pauses in speech give an indecisive or frightened person. The innocence of speech is very important in communication; sometimes, it is enough to understand what a person who speaks an unknown language wants to communicate. Paleolinguists believe that intonation as a means of communication originated even before the most complex speech.

Considering the main types of nonverbal means, it becomes clear not only how important they are, but also that they permeate all levels of communication literally. In interpersonal communication, they can completely replace words, and then people are told to understand each other without words. It happens that your partner is offended and angry, and you are confused to ask, "Well, what did I say to that, that you were offended?" So, he was not offended by 20% of the information you conveyed in words, but that 80% was shown by non-verbal means: intonation, facial expression, gaze, etc.

Verbal or non-verbal - what it is and what kind of communication is more important

Ancient beeps warned of danger or conveyed important information that a bush with edible berries was growing nearby.

Today, verbal communication is something that not every person can do without—starting with morning coffee for messengers to talking to colleagues at work about the boss's new relationship.

Differences between types of communication

Verbal and nonverbal communication

We learn to express our thoughts with the help of words; in school, they teach reading and writing. But speech and text are not the only possible ways we can convey information. The first in our lives, a natural and easy way to express thoughts, with the help of gestures and body language. Throughout life, we successfully combine these two methods of communication: verbal and nonverbal communication.

What is verbal communication

Verbal communication is the most well-known way for a person to transmit and receive information using oral or written language. Such communication takes place between two or more persons. To reproduce speech, a person has clear diction, a certain vocabulary, and knowledge of the rules of communication.

Vocabulary and syntax play an important role in the process of human communication through verbal communication. The first implies a certain set of words that belong to a certain language. The second dictates the rules of thought formation.

Verbal interaction has two important functions:

Which means. With the help of words, a person can present any description, and have an idea of the information received. The dictionary helps a person to analyze the received information, build connections between the objects about which the information was received, and distribute the degree of significance (most importantly, secondarily).

Communicative. Its task is to convey attitudes towards the information received or reproduced. When we speak, it is expressed through pauses, accents, the intonation of the voice, in the letter - correct spelling, punctuation, and text instructions.

Despite the greater importance of verbal communication in a person's life, it has several disadvantages:

- The inability to articulate one's thought clearly and bring it about.
- The complexity of the perception of another's narrative.
- Misunderstanding of received information.
- Multiple meanings of the same words.
- Language difficulties between bearers of different cultures, religions, ages, etc.

Scientists believe that verbal communication occupies a minimal, in terms of importance, place in human interaction skills. The quantitative utility index is only 15% compared to nonverbal skills. Science has given them 85% importance.

How to explain the term "nonverbal communication."

Nonverbal communication is the interaction between individuals without the use of words, linguistic methods of communication. To convey thoughts, emotions, a person, in this case, actively applies body language: gestures, facial expressions, posture, visual impact. Nonverbal communications can be unconscious, include the above methods of transmitting information and special. Others include language for the hearing impaired, deaf and dumb, and Morse code.

Body language helps a person create a connection between interlocutors, give meaning to words, and express emotions hidden in the text—the peculiarity of such communication insincerity. A person unfamiliar with the psychology of such communication is unable to control their emotions and body language. All non-verbal signs have their character: imaginary, open, insecure, friendly, belligerent, and suspicious.

It is important too! Understanding possible nonverbal cues give a person an advantage over the other person.

With such knowledge, the speaker can attract the attention of the public and adapt to their point of view. Business people and managers in important negotiations, using the language of the opponent's body, decide on his honesty and the correctness of the actions taken.

In conversation, posture, gestures, body language is of the utmost importance. Scientists have discovered that with differences in verbal and visual information, perceived by man, the latter will remain in the subconscious mind. With the help of nonverbal communication, the interlocutor can convince the correctness or subordinate his or her words to doubt.

Elements of the visual relationship include:

- Manner of holding (movement, action in a given situation).
- Emotional overtones (hand movements, facial expressions).
- Body contact (touch, handshake, hugs).
- Eye contact (student change, persistence, duration).
- Movement (walking, place of residence in one place).
- Reactions (response to some events).

Types of verbal and nonverbal communication

Verbal and nonverbal means of communication refer to methods of transmitting the information. Each of them, in turn, has a broad division into species.

Verbal communication involves presenting information using words, which are divided into the oral presentation and written speech. Each of them has subtypes. Oral speech includes:

Dialogue (exchange of information between one or more persons). Includes:

- Conversation - the exchange of information in the process of simple natural communication.
- Interview - an interactive process for obtaining certain professional information.
- Dispute - verbal exchange of information to clarify the situation, discuss the conflict.
- Discussions - reasoning in front of the audience to get a unified position on the difficult situation.
- Controversy - dispute using various scientific opinions.

Monologue - continuous performance of one person. That includes:

- Report - pre-prepared information based on journalistic, scientific materials.
- Lecture - comprehensive coverage of a particular problem of experts.
- Performance - a small presentation of

pre-prepared information on a particular topic.
- A message is a small analytical summary that contains fact-based information.

Written speech is divided into:

- Instant (transfer of textual information immediately after writing, followed by an early response).
- Delayed (response information is received after a long time or does not arrive at all).

Worth to mention! The tactile form of communication can be distinguished into a special category of verbal communication. Such communication is typical of people without hearing or sight. At the time of information transfer, they use a "handwritten letter."

Psychology studies, both verbal and nonverbal communication, allow the use of specific categories for the correct assessment of communication. As a result of many years of research, there are generally accepted ways of interpreting different forms of information transfer.

Nonverbal communication also has several types of communication. That includes:

- Kinesics - a set of body movements (gestures, postures, facial expressions, looks).
- Tactile acts - ways of touching another person.
- Sensory perception of the interlocutor from sensory organs (smells, tastes, color

- combinations, thermal sensations).
- Proxemics - communication takes into account the comfort zone (intimate, personal, social or public).
- Chronicle - use of temporary categories in communication.
- Paraverbal communication - transmission of certain rhythms during communication (the rhythm of voice, intonation).

Features of verbal communication

Verbal communication is characteristic only of human culture. Only people can express their thoughts in words. That is the main feature of this relationship. Also, you can mark:

- Diversity of styles (business, conversational, scientific, artistic and others).
- Exclusivity (words can describe any sign system).
- Ability to talk about a person (culture, level of knowledge, upbringing, character).
- Consolidation of expressions, phrases for certain cultures, social groups (fascism, communism, nihilism, democracy).
- The need for implementation in life (lack of verbal communication skills can be an insurmountable obstacle to personal and professional growth).

Features of nonverbal communication

The main feature of a nonverbal relationship is the complexity of controlling one's body movements, arms, facial expressions, and other important elements of such communication. Among other features of nonverbal communication note:

- Signal duality (body signs, movements that are accepted around the world are imitated, others will vary, depending on the culture of the population).
- Truthfulness (it is impossible to hide all signals that reflect real emotions completely).
- Creating a strong connection between the interlocutor (the whole picture helps people to gather a complete picture of the person, to shape their attitude towards him).
- Strengthening the meaning of words in verbal communication.
- The ability to explain the resulting thought before appropriate verbal descriptions appear.

How verbal and non-verbal communication helps in everyday life

Verbal and nonverbal interaction are integral parts of each other. Only a combination of these forms of communication gives us a complete picture of the information received. To communicate effectively with others, you must have skills in both of these areas.

Verbal and nonverbal communication briefly leave an impression on the person a few minutes after the start of communication. The level of oral and written language will speak to the culture and intellect level of the individual. Gestures and facial expressions will inform you about your emotional state and attitude towards the situation.

Speaking in public is not good enough to prepare a speech. The speaker must have public speaking skills. Certain speech building techniques allow the audience to become interested. But words alone are not enough. The speaker should be able to stay in public, make certain gestures, perform attention-grabbing movements, and entice the intonations of the voice.

Verbal and non-verbal means of business communication are inalienable knowledge of the top management of any company. In many countries, not only company directors but also ordinary managers need to know how a person behaves during ordinary communication, during interviews, and making important decisions.

By using gestures in the conversion process, a person can try to explain things that are difficult to reproduce in words. The interlocutor usually perfectly understands what they wanted to convey. Trying to talk to strangers, without enough vocabulary, people increase the color of their voice and actively gesture during communication. In teaching mathematics, explaining some functions, the lecturer can follow the words with a pattern in the air; for him, it is a way of visualizing words for the audience—a little help in understanding.

Man, resorts to various forms and methods of communication daily. That is our natural need. Verbal and non-verbal means of communication briefly provide an opportunity to form a certain opinion about the interlocutor, speaker, or opponent from the first minutes of communication. It is impossible to isolate any as the most important way of transmitting information. Both types of communication are informative and completely complementary.

Verbal and nonverbal communication

Communication is an integral part of every person's life. Thanks to the exchange of information, the expression of our thoughts, opinions, advice, and feelings, we can normally live in society, set goals for ourselves, and confidently approach their achievement.

Not always in disputes, friendly conversations, and simple exchange of information, interlocutors openly express their thoughts and feelings.

Verbal and non-verbal communication — these two components are inherent in the communication of each of us. Being able to recognize signs of nonverbal communication during a conversation makes it much easier for people to form a correct opinion about their environment.

The essence of verbal communication - what it is and why it is needed

Spoken communication means oral and written language. With their help, we can express our opinions and thoughts, honestly discuss with a companion, argue, share impressions with friends, and talk about what we have seen, heard, read, etc.

When one speaks, the other listens very carefully and responds responsibly. It can be an agreement, anger, a dispute, or just the absorption of new interesting information. Lack of verbal communication makes every person lonely, withdrawn, and isolated from the outside world. People come to compromise through disputes, explanations, and presentations of their thoughts and find a way out of difficult situations.

Proper speech is an important factor in verbal communication, which plays for the benefit of all. How quickly a person knows how to move in conversation, answer questions asked, make new connections, and express thoughts, his place in this world will depend directly. When applying for a job, the boss pays special attention to these factors.

In addition to simple words and sentences, the emotional message plays a particularly important role. By intonation, tone, speed of clarification, you can understand the mood of the interlocutor. Shouting, dissatisfaction, criticism often provoke a reaction in the form of aggression, ignoring the interlocutor. When the boss (friend, parents) chooses the words correctly and speaks calmly, it is easier for the employee to process the received information, find the mistake, and correct it.

Means of verbal communication

The main means of this communication is human speech. Thanks to spoken (written) words, people can convey their words and thoughts and learn new information. In addition to understanding and knowing the words, you need to be able to construct them correctly in a sentence and convey them to the interlocutor.

Such ways of verbal communication include:

- Intonation plays an important role in the communication process and helps to show your attitude about the current situation. For a more pleasant conversation, you need to be smooth and calm. In this case, all the data is more understandable and perceived by the listener.
- Voice quality is another important aspect. Of course, everyone has their tone and voice. But your training and ability to own it is a game for good. After all, there are often people with very loud or quiet voices naturally. This brings inconvenience in conversations because others have to listen or feel uncomfortable because of the noise. Unreliable people usually speak almost in whispers, quickly and swallowing the ending. Ambitious and goal-oriented people express expressions, loudly, and clearly.
- Speech speed is another tool that can say a lot about a person's feelings in a particular situation. The type of temperament also plays a significant role. Melancholic and phlegmatic, compared to a sanguine and choleric person, speak slowly.
- Logical and phrase stress allows each person to highlight the most important details in their story. Our perception of the information we hear

depends on putting the stress into words correctly.

What is nonverbal communication?

By ignoring the signs of nonverbal communication, people can make a big mistake. Many listen with their ears, even though the "body language" of the interlocutor is shouting the opposite.

Nonverbal language is expressed simultaneously in several forms, which differ from each other.

1. Chinese include pantomimes, facial expressions, and gestures. Very often, in emotional conversation, a person begins to wave their arms (movements), monkeys (mimicry), or assumes a closed pose with their arms crossed over their chests (pantomimes). Any subtle movements in the conversion process can be a sign of neglect, mistrust, arrogance, affection, or respect.

By learning to notice the little things and understand the mood of the interlocutor, you can avoid quarrels and unnecessary conflicts and wait for the right moment to achieve the goal and a calm mood. After all, very often, a person can see in what mood someone returned from work (or school). It can be a heavy, hunched gait, long silence, unwillingness to answer questions, or closed poses. If you approach a relative (friend) with reproaches and aggression for nothing, it is impossible to avoid an emotional response.

2. Takesika is another form of nonverbal communication. Without knowing its basics, conflicts and misunderstandings often occur between people. Touches are the main component of this type. Handshakes, hugs, pats on the shoulder, and more include taxa. Depending on how exactly these movements take place (distances, compression force, etc.), the mood or attitude of the person towards the interlocutor directly depends.

Very often in public transport at the time of the busiest traffic, people have to gather. In this case, many feel uncomfortable. Strong proximity due to crowds leads to people not intentionally invading each other's private space (range 115 to 45 cm). On a subconscious level, this is considered a danger and causes responses in the form of dissatisfaction, limitations.

3. The components of prosody are volume, intonation, and tilt of the voice. They are more recognizable and understandable signs for most people. Almost everyone knows what a raised voice and sharp intonation mean.

4. Extralinguistics - these are additional reactions during the conversation. These include laughter, sighs, incredible shouts, and pauses in speech.

Extralinguistics and judgment act as a complement to verbal communication. With their help, you can determine the mood and emotional state of the interlocutor.

Building relationships, taking into account the secrets of non-verbal communication:

In the process of communication, verbal and nonverbal types of communication are equally important for a person. Good orientation and understanding of "body language" will allow you to avoid deception, see the true feelings of your opponent, or hide your own. Speakers are specially educated and oriented to the principles of conversation and bilingual communication. Artists, philanthropists, politicians, and other speakers use self-control in all interviews and speeches. It helps not to reveal true thoughts and feelings and to avoid public condemnation.

Taking into account all the nuances of non-verbal communication and the correct recognition of its essence, each person will be able to understand the interlocutors, establish profitable relationships, and achieve their goals. The ability to speak correctly and attract listeners guarantees trust, a desire to cooperate and help.

Establish personal and business relationships or avoid fraud, deception - all this can be if you correctly recognize the message, which manifests itself on the interlocutor's subconscious level. Sometimes facial expressions, postures, and gestures speak many more words.

Top secrets to help you recognize a person's true emotions in the communication process:

1. Excessively intense gestures indicate emotional arousal. Too fast movements are a sign that the narrator is trying to give his best to the listener. Most often, friends talk similarly about their victories and achievements that have happened in their life situations.

It is important to note that a person's nationality and

temperament play a significant role in this factor. It is well known that Portuguese and Italians almost always use gestures in the conversation process. Finns are more reserved.

2. Many of us are used to reading emotions in the face of your interlocutor. Looking at the mimicry of friends, you can notice a lot of useful information.

Eye contact is an important element of any dialogue. How easy it is for people to look into their eyes, and the degree of their connection depends. With discomfort, deception, lies, and hypocrisy, a person always looks away or tries to avoid direct contact. A very long and close look at an unknown person or a stranger is evidence of a negative and aggressive attitude. In the process of communication, each participant in the conversation should be pleasant and simple.

3. Walking enters the pantomime and can say a lot about a person. Looking from the side, you can see the inner state and mood of the person walking. A raised head and a wide stride always testify to trust and a positive attitude. Shrugging of the shoulders, heavy movements of the legs, and a lowered appearance always speak of the opposite, namely - a bad mood, thoughtfulness, and concern. Being in anger, the gait is usually sudden and fast.

4. The position of the interlocutor is another very important point that can say a lot about the mood of the interlocutor to communicate his attitude towards the

narrator, and everything that happens. Everyone knows that arms crossed on your chest, speak of isolation, unwillingness to communicate, or share your opponents' points of view.

These little things play a significant role in the career-building process. After all, if during the discussion (project creation, distribution of duties) staff nod and agree, they are at the same time in a closed position - it is worth doubting their sincerity and desire for support.

By giving the person something to hold, you can push him to open it. One speaks of openness, honesty, and the desire to communicate when his body is turned and the free (not crossed) place of his legs and arms. To remove the discomfort during the promise, which is felt when you first meet, you can listen to a psychologist's advice and reflect on his positions, facial expressions, and gestures. So, you can join the wave of interlocutors and establish contact.

To reflect, that is, to repeat the pose, gestures, and facial expressions of the interlocutor. This way, you can get involved in one wave and facilitate communication.

5. A handshake can also say a lot about a man's relationship. Excessive compression indicates a person's authority and aggression. The barely visible squeezing of the fingers speaks of insecurity.

Win trust and win listeners, make them trust and make friends - all this is possible if you control your emotions and learn how to use non-verbal communication properly. Very often, the foundation of trust in the missions of sectarian churches, administrators, politicians, and speakers lies in their proper mood. Attitude, intonation, presentation of information, view - all these little things have special meanings in the process of speech, business negotiations, looking for investors, etc.

It can take years to learn how to control your feelings and prove it with nonverbal communication fully.

Why is knowledge of nonverbal communication so important in the modern world?

Often people misunderstand the feelings and intentions of their friends. In addition to body language, inner state or habits are also inherent. Not always a closed attitude indicates a bias towards the interlocutor. It happens that a person is not in the mood to engage in a cheerful discussion and share their thoughts. It all depends on emotions and inner spirit.

Therefore, the ability to notice all the little things and compare them with each other helps to find friends, understand relatives (acquaintances), not rush to conclusions and make the right opinion.

Internal features also play a significant role. Most people have their habits. Some are silent, and others twist their lips into a tube (bite them), raise their eyebrows, and so on. Such habits cannot be attributed to nonverbal communication and equated with personal relationships.

As you begin to learn the secrets of nonverbal communication and compare subconscious signals with spoken phrases, one should pay attention to one's behavior. After introspection, by observing how the body reacts to different phrases, people, and events, each person can understand others more adequately.

Being able to recognize (understand) body language, a person will be able to find true friends and like-minded people, achieve their goals, gain interest among listeners, and see negatively envious people, liars.

What exactly is verbal and nonverbal communication?

Communication is the most difficult process of interaction between people to achieve mutual understanding, gaining a certain experience. Every day a person rotates in society, establishes contacts with colleagues, households, friends. To achieve his goal in communication, a person uses verbal and non-verbal means.

Consider these two groups separately.

Verbal communication: language functions

Verbal communication is the use of words to convey information. The main tool is speech.

In communication, there are different goals: making a message, finding answers, criticizing opinions, encouraging action, reaching an agreement, etc. Depending on them, speech is built—orally or in writing—and implemented a language system.

Language is a set of symbols and means of their interaction that acts as an instrument for expressing feelings and thoughts. The language has the functions:

- Ethnic - the language of different nations has its own, which is their trademark.
- Constructive - adds thought to sentences, sound. When expressed verbally, it becomes clear and distinct. The speaker can evaluate it from the side - what effect it produces.
- Cognitive - expresses the activity of consciousness. A person gets the most knowledge about the surrounding reality through communication, language.
- Emotional - colors of thought using intonation, timbre, diction features. The function of language works in moments when the speaker is trying to convey a certain emotion.
- Communicative language as the main way of communication. It provides a complete exchange of information between people.
- Contact setting - meeting and maintaining contacts between subjects. Sometimes communication does not carry a specific goal, does not contain useful information, and plays an important role in further relationships. It also serves as a basis for building trust.
- Accumulative - through language, a person collects, and stores acquired knowledge. The subject gets the information, wants to remember it in the future. An effective way is to record the minutes or keep a diary, but the appropriate paper media is not always at hand. Word transmission by mouth is also a good method for

assimilating information. Although the book, in which everything is structured and subordinated to a certain goal, the meaning is, of course, the most valuable source of important data.

Speech activity: language forms

Speech activity - a situation in which communication between people takes place through verbal components of language. There are different types:

- A letter is a fixation of the content of a speech on paper or electronic media.
- Speech is the use of language to convey a message.
- Reading - the visual perception of information recorded on paper or computer.
- Listening is the audio perception of information from speech.

Based on the spoken form, communication is oral and written. And if we consider this depending on the number of participants, it can be divided into a mass, interpersonal.

Both literary and non-literary forms of language are different for each nationality, and they determine the nation's social and cultural status. Literary language is exemplary and structured, with stable grammatical norms. It is also presented in two forms: oral and written. The first is a speech that sounds, and the second can be read. In this case, the oral speech appeared earlier, and it was a source that people began to use: non-literary speech - dialects of individual nations and territorial features of oral language.

But the most important thing in the psychology of communication is non-verbal communication. The person unconsciously uses various signs: gestures, facial expressions, intonation, posture, position in space, etc. Let us continue to consider this extensive group.

Nonverbal communication

Nonverbal communication is "body language." One does not use speech, but uses other means that enable him to perform important functions:

- Emphasizing the importance. Without mentioning superfluous words, a person may use a gesture or take a certain attitude that indicates the importance of the moment.
- Contradictory. The speaker says a few words but thinks the exact opposite. For example, a clown on stage is uncomfortable and unhappy in life. The slightest mimicry movements on his face will help you understand that as well as exposing a lie if a person wants to hide behind an insincere smile.
- Sometimes each of us follows enthusiastic words with a gesture or movement, indicating the strong emotionality of this situation.
- Instead of words. The subject uses clear gestures and saves time. For example, shrugging or direction should not require further clarification.

- Repeat and amplify the effect of speech. An oral call is sometimes very emotional, and nonverbal means are designed to emphasize the strength of your statement. Nodding your head with the appropriate answer "Yes" or "No" signifies trust and intransigence.

Types of nonverbal means

A large group of kinesthetic - external manifestations of feelings, emotions of a person during communication. This is:

Gestures and pictures

Interlocutors evaluate each other long before the conversation begins. Posture, gait, gaze can give, in advance, a person's uncertainty or, conversely, self-confidence, with claims to power. Gestures usually emphasize the meaning of speech, give it an emotional nuance, put accents, but their abundance can also spoil the impression, especially at a business meeting. Also, in different nationalities, the same gestures mean opposite phenomena.

Intense gestures determine a person's emotional state. If his movements intersect, there are a lot of them, and then the subject is overly excited, and overly interested in passing his information to the opponent. This can be both a plus and a significant disadvantage depending on the circumstances.

Pose plays no less of a role. If the subject has crossed his arms, he is skeptical and doesn't trust you much. Perhaps closed, unwilling to communicate in principle. If the interlocutor turned his body towards you, did not cross his arms and legs, then, on the contrary, he was open and ready to listen. In psychology, for effective communication, it is recommended to deflect the opponent's attitude to achieve relaxation and trust from him.

Gest

A person's face is the main source of information about his inner state. A dark forehead or smile is a factor that determines further communication with the subject. The eyes reflect the human essence. There are seven types of basic emotions, each of which has its characteristic signs: anger, joy, fear, sadness, longing, surprise, disgust. They are easy to remember, identify, and observe in people to understand the moods of others better.

Pantomime

This may include walking. A closed person or a frustrated person is often scared, lowers his head, does not look into his eyes, but likes to look at his feet. Angry people walk with sharp movements, they hurry, but they are heavy. A confident and cheerful person has an elastic gait or a long stride. It varies depending on the health condition.

There is a part of non-verbal means, taking into account the distance between the speakers—proxemics. Determines the comfortable distance between the interlocutors. There are several areas of communication:

Intimate - 15-45 cm, here, the person recognizes only

those closest to him. The invasion of unknown personalities can be understood as a threat that requires immediate protection.

Personally - 45-120 cm, valid for good friends, colleagues.

Social and public - typical for business negotiations, important events, and speeches from the stands.

Takesika is a communication section dedicated to the role of touch. If it is wrong to apply them, without considering the differences in social status, age, field, you can get into an awkward situation, even causing conflict. Handling is the safest touch—particularly characteristic of men who check their opponents' strength through it. Choose, so to speak, which of them is the most dominant. Sometimes insecurity, or disgust, or flexibility is easily given when a person shakes only one's fingertips.

Voice characteristics

Intonation, volume, tone, the rhythm of the voice can serve as an example of a combination of two types of communication. The same sentence will sound completely different if you alter the above methods. The meaning and effect on the listener depend on it. There may also be pauses, laughter, and sighs, which are colored with additional colors.

It is important to understand that a person unknowingly transmits to his opponent using non-verbal means, more than 70% of the information. The receiving entity must interpret correctly to avoid misunderstandings and quarrels. The observer also appreciates the signals sent to the speaker, and perceives them emotionally, but interpreting all this is not always correct.

Also, a person speaks orally only 80% of what he originally intended to convey. The opponent listens carefully, distinguishes only 60%, and then forgets ten percent of the information. Therefore, it is very important to consider nonverbal cues to at least remember the purpose, the meaning of the recipient's message you wanted to convey.

5 NLP Techniques You Must Master

Correct and timely clues are enough to change the route of your life completely. Well, here you will find as many as five fresh tips.

1. Logical levels of perception

Although this is not a technique, a model of levels of perception, everyone needs to "walk" in it at least several times in life. The fact is that not only firms and society are built at these levels, but also our inner world, and we know that the inside is the outside.

"Walking" through logical levels, you will discover a lot of new things about yourself: who you are, where you are on the life span, whether you are far from the point you want to come to. And if somewhere there was a veil in front of your eyes, then after it will subside, and your life will appear before you in its true form.

These levels are arranged hierarchically, where each higher-level controls the lower ones, making them look like a pyramid. The higher the level, the stronger its influence on our lives and each level has its own "zone of responsibility" and asks the person his questions. It is to these questions that you need to answer yourself.

- **Level number 1. Environment**

Questions: Who am I? What do I look like? What do I have? Where do I live, work, relax? When do I live? What kind of people surround me (with whom I spend time)?

It is this level that we, first of all, begin to redraw when "everything is bad": we buy new clothes, change our hairstyles, go on a trip, meet new people, make repairs, etc. Often such "cosmetic changes" really bring improvement, the main thing here is to treat them with problems at the same level.

- **Level number 2. Behavior**

Questions: What do I do every day? What can I do? What do I want to be able to? What do I want to do?

This is the level of action, and it is on it that it is most useful to set goals for the result. For example: "do English every day for 20 minutes," "call mom," "write a report."

The results at this level determine the results at the first level: we are what we do every day.

- **Level number 3. Abilities**

Questions: What can I do? What do I want to learn?

This is the level of our skills abilities. It rises above the previous two and determines the results on them: we have the results of what we do, but we do what we can. When we learn something new, we begin to do something new, and, accordingly, we begin to receive something new.

As the saying goes, "To have something you never had, you must do something you've never done."

Answer yourself honestly, what skills do you have and what do you want to develop? It can be anything: the ability to get along with people, play the guitar, write code, learn fast.

- **Level number 4. Values and Beliefs**

<u>Questions</u>: What is the most important thing for me in life (what are my values)? What is the world like (what are my beliefs about my values)?

Manipulations at this level are corrected immediately by the three previous levels. This is what we consider the most important, and according to which laws for us, "this is important" works. For example, if one of your values is family, then you subconsciously have a list of unspoken rules about it: "family is the greatest happiness," "the sooner you start a family, the better," "if the family has problems, then everything else does not matter," etc.

Beliefs determine how we achieve our values and whether we achieve them at all. They are like the frame on which the world is built in our head, and the only difference is that for some, it is a frame for the castle, while for others, it is for the hut.

- **Level number 5. Identity**

<u>Questions:</u> Who am I? (better - in different contexts of life: at work, in sex, in the family, etc.)

This is also a matter of conviction, only now not about the world, but oneself. All these "I'm a woman, I should not work so hard!" or "I am a true specialist," "I am a great mom" - issues of identity. Throughout life, a person acquires new diverse identities, which form many results at all previous levels.

We are woven from many identities that "guide" the different contexts of our lives. They are like voices in the head that tell a person who he is and what he can. Answer yourself, who are you?

- **Level 6. Mission**

<u>Questions:</u> Why am I doing what I am doing? For what more?

This is the only level that affects something more than the interests and desires of a person, and they are subject to the interests and desires of the whole world. Here the influence of a person by his actions on the world and people around him is determined; this is the level of interaction between man and the world. Therefore, answering yourself questions of this level, you influence almost everything in your life. Often the answers to this question force people to change their whole path radically.

2. "Well-formulated result"

This technique in NLP is always and everywhere used for setting goals. It's a shame that it is widely known only in narrow circles, because, setting goals for it is the only right option in which your goals are realized by themselves. Sabotage and procrastination leave a person simply rolling toward the goal, like a bowling ball.

Why does it happen? It's just that the "KhSR" technique allows you to neutralize the only personified person and, concurrently, your main enemy—your brain. Special formulations help to reach your limbic system (unconscious) and connect it with the neocortex (consciousness). It is precisely the coordinated work of these two guys that is the key to achieving all goals.

3. "I'm the other way around"

This is also a powerful technique that will enrich your picture of the world with experience, wisdom, and new resources. Having done it, you will feel how much easier it became for you to do what was previously given with a creak, you look at your problems and complex tasks in work or communication from a new angle.

The essence of the technique is as follows: you need to "turn on" your opposite for several hours, and all this time think and act based on it.

For instance. There you are—an active, opportunity person. You like to see life in wide, large strokes, without bothering with the details. You make decisions in your life because you know that your decisions are the best.

And now they say to you: now, dear friend, stay with yourself for several hours with a reflective, thoughtful, slow brake. And do not see opportunities everywhere! Replace strategy with tactics and procedures. Turn on meticulousness. And more, more attention to detail!

Or vice versa: you, all so procedural, thoughtful, doubting, and attentive to details, will transform into an active, large-scale, decisive person who decides to trifle with an internal reference. Perhaps even with signs of a tyrant. Why not? After all, the medal always has two sides.

I warn you, and the first thought will be: "What a horror! How can one live like that?" And then ... Then a new model of behavior spreads heat throughout the body, and you become so unusually good and interesting. And the boundaries of the possible are being pushed.

In both cases, you will learn very, very much.

Often—exactly what you are missing.

4. Creative Walt Disney Strategy

This approach is indispensable for a good result (or at least minimizing losses) for both your business projects and simply multifactor ideas like moving or changing jobs. It gained popularity because it was used each time by Walt Disney and his team to create cartoons. And given their fantastic popularity, this is more than a self-sufficient argument in favor of the method, agree?

The bottom line is to think about a task/project with three roles:

- Dreamer
- Realist
- Critic

Dreamer looks at the idea through the prism of endless possibilities. He describes all the most amazing results, the most daring desires, gives out the most daring and absurd ideas. Imagine that your resources are not limited, and you can realize any of your whims, and start writing down your wildest fantasies, the most beautiful result.

At this stage, it is better to glue the mouth of the cynical part of your personality in advance—she will still have time to speak out. Now let yourself go on a fantasy flight, where your possibilities are endless.

Being in this state of mind, ask yourself the following questions:

- "What do I want?"
- "What is the ideal option?"
- "What benefit will it bring when it is realized?"
- "What opportunities will come with implementation?"

A realist looks at an idea in terms of numbers. He studies the market and all the components that can affect the equation's outcome to sensibly calculate how many resources will be needed to implement the idea. He evaluates expectations and reality to find a compromise.

If the dreamer thought strategically, then the realist's paraphyly is a tactic. It makes a step-by-step route of optimal movement to the plan.

Thinking like a realist, find answers to the following questions:

- "How much time will I need?"
- "How much money will I need?"
- "What knowledge and skills do I need?"
- "Who can help me in achieving and how to persuade them to do this?"

The critic must look at the task with eyes filled with doubt. Here you play the role of the prosecutor, look out for all possible and impossible pitfalls, difficulties that you have to stumble on and assess the height of the barriers you have to jump.

These are the questions you need to answer yourself honestly:

- "What can hinder implementation or slow it down?"
- "What does this project look like for a client? What might he not like about it?"
- "At what stage can something go wrong, and why?"
- "If an idea is realized, what will it rob me of? What will I sacrifice?"
- "Who can be against this idea, and why? How can I get around this resistance?"
- "Is it worth it?"

5. "Change in personal history"

If traumatic events have happened in your life against

which complexes or anxiety have grown in you, then this technique is for you. It works great when you need to work on:

- Childhood grievances, unsuccessful experiences (disgraced, failed, offended, etc.)
- The repeated negative situation, "on the same rake."
- Toxic beliefs leading to difficulties ("after 40 there is no life", "you won't earn much money," "not with my happiness," etc.)

Remember, you do not need to work through this technique for injuries associated with the care of loved ones or physical violence (if any) if you have not undergone NLP practice or are not under the supervision of a professional. Take something simpler, preferably from childhood.

The main idea of this technique is this: any negative event injures us only when we do not have enough resources to deal with it. Therefore, to remove the traumatic effect, you need to give yourself these resources in the past.

The bottom line is: You "enter" an unpleasant memory and change it for the better, giving yourself the resources, you need for this past. Resources—this is exactly what you did not have then, to live this situation easily, to get out of it as a winner. Therefore, almost anything will be a resource: support, money, indifference, self-confidence, sense of humor, arrogance, beauty, and so on.

CHAPTER 12

STOICISM FOR LIFE

What's Stoicism?

Stoicism is the ability or the willpower of an individual to control their feelings or emotions. Someone stoic, therefore, stands firm in the face of adversity. For example: "The woman showed stoicism in the face of the tragedy," "You have to have stoicism at the business level if you want to progress," "When I had to be left out of the team, I accepted it with stoicism."

The notion of Stoicism is also used to refer to a philosophical school founded by the Greek Zenon de Citio some three hundred years before Christ. Stoic doctrine promoted the mastery of the passions that generate disturbances, appealing for this to reason and personal virtue.

According to Stoicism, the key to happiness is found in ataraxia: the balance that is achieved when there are no troubles. To achieve ataraxia, the individual must remain oblivious to material vicissitudes and must refrain from making judgments.

Stoicism doubted the existence of sensitive knowledge since perception depends on the subject. Therefore, given the various situations that the same person is going through or the factors that affect the object, it is impossible for there to be an immediate reproduction of a thing.

The Stoic, therefore, intended to live according to reason and free from passions. Stoicism was invited to dominate the reactions through self-control since Stoicism understood love as a deviation from the rational nature of the human being. So, he fostered a life in tune with natural laws.

One of the current figures of Stoicism is the professor of philosophy, Massimo Pigliucci, born in Italy in 1964, who works in the North American university system called City University of New York. In his book, "How to be Stoic", published by the Ariel publishing house, he offers us a series of tips to take advantage of this current of thought born three centuries before Christ to live better.

According to Pigliucci, there is no single way or group of doctrines to follow to respect the foundations of Stoicism, and this differentiates it from certain religions. Stoics move through life, combining a series of practices and techniques that they find in their own experience, and thus they build their paths individually.

To experience Stoicism in the 21st century, the author offers specific "spiritual exercises" that we can apply in our day-to-day activities:

* **Temperance:** It is a reflection about the fleeting nature of things. This should be practiced with a particular focus on the things that are most precious to you, those that benefit us the most or that we value the most, to

understand that everything and everyone ceases to exist sooner or later.

* **Anticipation:** It is good to contemplate the potential consequences of our plans, to avoid being surprised. In this way, we will have more control over stressful situations.

* **Self-control:** We should not be complicit in those who try to hurt us since their provocation can only work if we allow it. The impulses can lead to our destruction, and we must control them trying to think cold just before taking significant decisions.

* **Solidarity:** Stoicism seeks a harmonious life with our environment, and that is why it proposes to empathize with the pain of others as if it were our own.

* **Observation:** The human being tends to give opinions much more frequently than to observe in silence, which prevents him from enriching himself. It is imperative to find the content before sharing it, to say only things that can serve some purpose, instead of spending saliva and energy covering the silence, one of our most valuable resources.

The quick guide to understanding the Stoics

Stoicism was one of history's most influential doctrines. When we learn that someone is approaching it "with the theory," it's generally because under the Stoics' teachings they face life, and that's because this philosophical movement has some methods to make it simpler for us, if not to solve it. For those who want to get closer to it, here's a short description.

If there is an ideology that has succeeded in dazzling people of all circumstances and ages, it is Stoicism. This branch of thought, whose foundation we owe to Zenón de Citio, would remain at the forefront of philosophical culture for no less than half a millennium (from the 3rd century BC to the 2nd century AD) and would maintain influence throughout the following centuries as history has rarely seen. We are going to review here its most outstanding characteristics that perhaps explain the reason for such success.

One philosophy, two proper names

As we have said, the founder of Stoicism was Zenón de Citio, a disciple of Crates de Tebas. He developed his thinking from the cynical theses of his teacher (hence the precise harmony between both philosophies in various aspects).

However, who made Stoicism a relevant doctrine was Chrysippus of Solos, who directed the Stoa (the Stoic school, located on the painted portico of Athens) from 232 BC. C. to 204 A. C. Thanks to his enormous dialectical talent and his gigantic production—nothing less than 700 works, of which sadly only fragments have reached us—Chrysippus managed not only that Stoicism was a highly relevant philosophy, but that the Stoa arrived to overcome Plato's Academy and Aristotle's Lyceum.

Although there were other renowned philosophers in this school—such as Cleanthes, Panetius, Posidonius, and his most famous disciple, Cicero—we would have to wait for the Roman Empire for the new batch of philosophers of enormous fame to arrive, with Seneca, Epictetus and the emperor philosopher Marco Aurelio.

Man, and his morals, main concern

The center of the Stoics' study is self-explanatory: man. Everything of his philosophy is for man, and more importantly, his morals. At the service of the individual, philosophy, physics, and ethics pose an objective that never seems to lose direction: to teach us to live according to our nature.

The Stoics accept two principles: matter and reason. But in fact, the latter is not something different; we can find it all over the place. According to the Stoics, rationality and Nature are identified, as Nature is the creator of the universe and its substance at the same time. It is because of this that we can assume the world's existence is moral.

Everything, so to speak, is bound by natural law, a universal basis. A union that also embraces man, linking him to the universe, as he is a logical being as well. All of this system shapes an inexorable chain of already-established relationships, triggers, and consequences that we perceive as fate. And stoics are deterministic. They believe the world's events are pre-established, and we can do very little to change them.

Autarchy: to be happy with self-sufficiency

Like the cynics, the Stoics find that the sage's goal is to ensure that he does not need anything to make life complete. So how does that joy come to be? To live by our moral existence, that is to say, to live virtuously.

Since the sage lives and is correctly decided in harmony with the world, the Stoic ideal is the one Epictetus expressed to us: assistance and resignation. Support it, because your fate will be the same whether or not you like it. It's a divinity-established scheme you can't run from, so we have no choice but to obey it meekly or let it take us away. Giving up, because finding peace will always be easier for us, and with it the desired happiness, if our impulses and appetites do not overpower us. If we have few needs and know how to regulate our emotions, it will be very easy to live happily, hence the value of both laws.

All inside and nothing outside

The point of departure for Stoic ethics is that true happiness depends only upon ourselves. What makes stoic an impregnable character is these ideas. Everything outside matters to him, because all his efforts are to attain goodness, what depends on him, what no one can take from him... Inside. That's the secret to their might.

The Stoic is not afraid of something, no matter how bad things go, as he has achieved ataraxia, the imperturbability of mind. This concept, in the same way, is the ultimate goal that Buddhists seek to attain enlightenment. Due to its existence, the stoic thus continues to live in utter harmony. Neither feelings, nor joy, nor pain or riches has control over a man who accepts his destiny and only cares about living virtuously. The Stoic puts himself above material objects and is fully autonomous, focusing on his inner life.

A sensualist theory

The theory of knowledge of the Stoics starts, like that of Aristotle, the empiricists, or the positivists, from sensible experience. That is to say, of the senses. For the Stoics, it is a process that goes through different stages. In the first place, what comes to us through the senses leaves a representation (an impression, says Zeno) in our reason, which, as we have already said, is the part of "divinity" that we possess and which connects us with the rationality of nature. However, these representations are not yet knowledge. If we simply accepted that as a sample of reality, we would not be before expertise, but before an opinion. For it to become knowledge, that representation must have evidence that invites intelligence to accept it. That consent must be given by hegemonikon, the Self. Understanding comes when the data that the senses offer us pass through the sieve of rationality.

Cosmopolitan

The Stoics, unlike the Cynics, did not despise their peers or society. To the cynic, all those who lived wrongly were only fools, who deserved to be insulted and ridiculed for their stupidity. An architect of it was Diogenes, famous for his rifirrafes with subjects of all fur. However, the cynical acid criticism did not try to correct or serve as an example to his fellow men but was content to belittle them.

The Stoics, for their part, have this critical vision, but they do not share the form. In fact, for them, the idea of community is fundamental. Now, faithful to their thinking and their belief that the fine thread of rationality unites the world, they considered themselves citizens of the world. They did not believe in being here or there for reasons of birth or culture. They were of reason and virtue wherever they reigned.

Four keys to building your resilience

Daily life is peppered with difficulties, small and large obstacles that must be learned to overcome. None of us came into this world with a manual of perfect existence, the one that gives us guidelines for each problem, for each crisis and each difficulty. Therefore, it is essential to develop your resilience. Only then can you face all the adversities that may surprise you in life.

We come into this world like fallen from a strange fireplace called destiny, luck or providence. We are offered a family more or less useful, a society more or less democratic, which grows with certain norms and values, and a social circle in which we create ourselves as we grow.

Continuous growth

As growing people that we are, it is always worth learning from all those trends that come our way, and that can offer us improvement mechanisms. And resilience is one of them, and it is nothing more or less than the ability to face problems and adapt as well as possible to those bumps, to those curves in the form of losses, failures, disappointments, trauma, and even stressful situations.

We must be clear, being resilient does not mean at all, not feeling discomfort, emotional pain, or difficulty in the face of adversity. Resilience is the ability to take the pain, accept it, and learn from it. At the same time, we manage both our emotions and our responses to cope with adversity in the best possible way.

It is not easy, we know, learning to be resilient is a long process that requires time and a lot of self-knowledge. But once mastered and understood, we will feel more capable and more protected. Let's see then the strengths and some keys to develop your resilience.

1. Insight ability

The first of the keys to building your resilience is understanding yourself. For this, knowing how to listen to yourself and speaking with that inner voice connected with that nervous skein of feelings and emotions will be essential. To achieve this, stop and simply attend to that inner rumor that shapes you as a vulnerable and also strong person.

It is the ideal time to practice mindfulness. This technique will allow you to attend to your thoughts. A fundamental aspect is not to judge any thought that crosses your mind. We just have to watch them and let them go like clouds in the sky. In this way, little by little, we will investigate within ourselves and meet the demons that torment us. So, as we get to know each other, we will be able to face situations much more calmly and deeply.

2. Essential motivation

Adversity can embrace you with its cold and terrible cloak. He will want to take your breath away and plunge you into a lonely corner. But you must not let yourself be defeated. There are many other things beyond pain, loss, or frustration. Your project, your need to keep going, to hope again for life and yours. We all must have an existential plan, a goal on the horizon for which to continue smiling every morning.

From Buddhist psychology, they defend that adversity should serve as an impulse to learn. Both good and evil can be determined. Therefore, instead of looking at problems as a hindrance in our lives, we see them as a possibility of personal development. Without a doubt, we will be opting for an option that will remarkably enrich us.

3. Emotional self-regulation

It is good that you feel the anger, the pain, the grief, the sadness... it is essential to cry and let off steam. But once we have passed this stage, it is time to get up and regulate these emotions, rationalizing them first towards acceptance and then towards overcoming.

Know your feelings, accept them, and guide them towards an optimal and healing process that manages to strengthen you. Knowing how you feel at each moment is the first step to know yourself deeply. This way, you will develop your resilience.

4. Positive attitude and self-confidence

It is not just a label. It is not that phrase that sells so much and that you find so many times on the walls of your social networks: Maintaining a positive attitude towards life is a necessity. We know that sometimes it is not easy, that darkness devastates us without anyone expecting it, without anyone having prepared for it and that it may be impossible to show a smile in such circumstances.

But rest assured that no dawn could be overcome at dusk, and what seems so black to you today will gradually lose that intensity if you face it with strength and optimism. And above all, with confidence in yourself.

Being rich depends on your state of mind

How to get rich and live happily achieving financial freedom? Through a model with which to be happy, in addition to reaching our job and economic goals. One of the secrets to making the human being happy depends to a greater extent on his mental state and that of the people around him.

It all starts with the dreams and goals that each person has, depending on age, personal situation, purchasing power, the lifestyle they can lead. Whoever tries to kill our thoughts does so because first, they have stopped believing in theirs. In reality, you should not merely dream of becoming rich: you must do everything possible to improve, learn, and expand as individuals. For this reason, we must define ourselves. We must also bear in mind that we will follow the most appropriate path to achieve the objectives that we set ourselves whenever we are ourselves.

What I have learned in recent years is that success has no secrets. It has a simple recipe, which is made up of determination, continuous training, techniques, and correct psychology. If I have to give a percentage, I would say that psychology represents 80%, because it allows you to see opportunities where there are problems. People overestimate what they can do in 1 year and underestimate what they can do in 5 years. Focusing on what you want is one of the keys to success for people who get results.

It is essential to have a mindset ready to make sacrifices to achieve the proposed goals. Even so, it could be understood that problems with money are not linked to the class to which each person belongs. Paradoxically, those with a lot of money have much bigger problems to solve.

Surely among the goals that make you happy is not to work all day and get home tired, and you do not feel like doing anything else. You may want to have more free time and more money to spend more time with your family and friends, dedicate yourself to a new hobby or fulfill one of those dreams ... who is preventing you from achieving this goal? Although this lifestyle may seem unattainable, it will only be feasible if we become financially free.

Money is only an amplifier that works by increasing what

you already are. It will give you more chances, more freedom, more choice, but money alone cannot make you happy. Only an excellent psychological approach to things and people, together with the ability to manage events and moods, will make you happy. You want the results, but the results depend on your actions. And on what do your steps depend? Of the state of mind, you are in. And the ability to locate yourself in a particular state of mind allows you to develop actions that lead you to specific results.

When I first started dealing with money, I underestimated the implications of using the body for managing moods and money in particular. In reality, behind any performance, there are types of breathing and use of the body itself, such that through a specific position and breathing in a certain way, the mind's productive states can be accessed.

It is essential to know what position money occupies in the hierarchical scale of our life. And the correct hierarchical level should be:

1. People
2. Money
3. Things

In this way, those people who put money before other people will not be more productive. Human beings and interpersonal relationships come first than any number. It is having good relationships with people that makes us truly rich. In the second place, we find money. With it, you can buy things, but with words, you can't necessarily buy money. With money, I can buy a car, but with that car, once I am out of the dealership, I cannot get the same amount of money.

How have we learned to walk? Falling, rising and falling again, until we managed to stay on our feet. The same thing happens to someone who wants to get rich. To achieve this, you have to do something that you like and take moments of rest so that in this way, your mental health accompanies your dreams and motivations, with which you will finally achieve that financial freedom that we long for.

The Most Important Stoic Philosophers

The term stoic originates in the term stoicism. Today these terms mean an aversion to all feelings, whether it's excruciating joy, hate or a kind of impassivity passion. The stoicism philosophy, though, is completely new and follows a very new range of concepts.

With time, the philosophy of stoicism developed particularly with the coming of Rome, the original philosophy was rendered in Athens by a Greek philosopher called Zeno of Citium. The more prominent stoic philosophers may be Seneca (the younger) and Marcus Aurelius (Rome's stoic emperor).

The basic teachings of stoicism are that bad emotions come from bad judgment, and the core of stoicism is to overcome these destructive emotions through control. They also say that true happiness is achieved through virtue. Stoics presented the philosophy as a way of life through which you can become a sage.

A sage is someone who has achieved ethical and intellectual perfection. Many philosophers (including Seneca) emphasized the belief that happiness is achieved through virtue. With this being true, a sage would be immune to misfortune since misfortune causes unhappiness, and through virtue, there is no unhappiness. This gives a powerful sense of controlling one's fate.

Stoicism also concerns itself heavily with fate and human free will. They believe in determinism (the idea that all future events are controlled by all past events in philosophy similar to fate), but they also believe in individual free will. This mixture of belief produces both a sense of acceptance of what will be while still trying to change the future for the better.

One of the virtues that stoicism talks about is control. One has to be in control of themselves, and many stoic philosophers talk of how a wicked man is like a dog tied to a cart, and he will go where he will go, but a stoic or virtuous man will go where he chooses. The set of virtues that stoicism talks of are not religious ethics, to say that God laid down a set of rules and will be unhappy if you break these rules. But rather a set of naturalistic ethics. That is even if there is no afterlife, you should still be a good person simply because it is good to be a good person.

Stoicism also puts a lot of importance on the idea of logic.

They believe that only through logic and truth can knowledge be attained. Though this seems common logic in today's society, it is important to look back then when the temples told you why a storm had blown in and why the stars had the patterns they had.

One of the greatest lines of stoicism is as follows. Quoted from Marcus Aurelius. "Say to yourself in the early morning: I shall meet today ungrateful, violent, treacherous, envious, uncharitable men. All of these things have come upon them through ignorance of real good and ill... I can neither be harmed by any of them, for no man will involve me in the wrong, nor can I be angry with my kinsman or hate him, for we have come into the world to work together".

Thinking Like a Stoic

There are several ways to understand philosophy. From understanding the three stoic disciplines to building everything on the principle of living according to nature to deriving the stoic principles from his vision of the physical, logical, and ethical foundations.

Thinking about philosophy from different points of view has innumerable advantages, both practical and theoretical.

In this section, we will suggest a simple mnemonic that is related to the first principle: Ignorance of external action. The four Aces: acceptance, conscience, action, and antifragility.

Stoic acceptance

Stoic acceptance is about accepting what is out of your control. Human minds are prone to agonize over the future or the past. We can spend hours ruminating on completely fictitious events. Seneca reminds us to stay in the present. What is out of our hands we can accept.

True happiness is enjoying the present, without anxiously depending on the future. Not to have fun with hopes or fears, but resting satisfied with what we have, which is enough for the one who has nothing.

When we are agitated by what is beyond our control, we are stealing time. We are distracting ourselves from living by our values.

However, it is too easy to desire impossible things. How do you handle this? Marcus reminds us: "When you face someone else's shamelessness, ask yourself this: Is a world without shameless possible? No. Then don't ask the impossible."

Importantly, this does not mean suppressing negative emotions. When we fight negative emotions, they can arise with a vengeance. Instead, we can accept that we will experience negative emotions and direct our attention to what matters.

We can expect things to go wrong in the external and internal world (feelings, emotions, personality, actions, principles, and values). Will it be difficult? The Stoic can accept difficulties and move on.

Stoic Consciousness

Stoic consciousness is based on stoic acceptance. The crucial idea is that it is our mind that causes us suffering. Instead of getting caught, we can take responsibility for our thoughts and actions.

When we lack consciousness, we pay attention to what others think of us, our state, and the external that is in our control. However, these things are not the true cause of our suffering. It is our value judgments that cause us suffering. We would not be held hostage to what others think of us if we did not believe that another person's value judgment is important. Instead, we must focus on what is under our control, our thinking, and our actions. YOU CAN TRAIN YOUR MIND, and THIS IS THE GREAT NEWS.

Epictetus mentions the following, pay attention:

Practice saying to each harsh appearance, "YOU ARE AN APPEARANCE, AND IN NO WAY WHAT YOU SEEM TO BE."

Taking control of our thinking means embracing reality. We are prone to adding value judgments and additional stories to whatever happens to us. This can be helpful, but it often clouds our judgments. We are especially vulnerable when we forget that our thoughts are not reality, that the stories we tell ourselves are often false, and that they retain control over their thoughts.

Stoic action

The previous two themes of Stoicism focused on the

mind. Action discipline is about acting in the world. Both disciplines are useless if not combined with the correct action. Marco Aurelio tells us: "Don't waste any more time arguing about what a good man should be, be one."

We have control over our characters. Over time, through small actions, we build habits. It is up to us to act wisely, moderately with courage and justice. We are responsible for our actions. Our actions should never depend on other people.

It can be easy to get distracted with our colleagues, the media, daily circumstances, and forget everything mentioned. This is why acceptance and stoic awareness are so important to the action. What matters is what you do.

Stoic antifragility

Finally, the Stoics were antifragile. Rather than simply being resilient and surviving, the famous Stoics were driven by stressors. This led Nassim Taleb to label the Stoics as "Buddhists with an attitude."

What antifragility does is that it helps us get out of our heads. We are waiting for negative action, instead of asking, "How can I make this go away?" Let us ask, "How can I use this to drive action?" And then we act.

It is important to accept what we cannot change, but it is also important to ingeniously seek the good, whatever the obstacles. Don't lean too much towards the acceptance side.

Each of these aspects of stoicism: acceptance, awareness, action, and anti-fragility are mutually related. A person can go much deeper in a certain aspect.

How to Become a Warrior-Philosopher

Japanese culture is millennial, and throughout its history, it has given great value to the virtues in combat. Unlike what happens in other latitudes, the Japanese fighter must be full of values to be worthy. The word bushido speaks precisely of this and is translated as the warrior's path.

This warrior path, or bushido, talks about a code of ethics that samurai applied. It contains a series of principles, but above all, seven values, which should govern behavior. It is said that members of the ruling class were taught from an early age.

The code name samurai also know the warrior's path. This condenses principles of Buddhism, Confucianism, and other Eastern philosophies. It is still a valuable guide to life. These are the seven virtues and teachings that it exalts.

1. Courage, an indispensable virtue of being free

According to the way of the warrior, only when you have courage can you be free. It is the courage that allows us to live fully, without the bonds that fear imposes. It takes courage to decide to act, especially to do great things.

Courage is not blind fearlessness. For it to be true courage, it must be accompanied by intelligence and strength. Fear exists, but we must not allow ourselves to be overcome by it. Instead, we should replace it with caution and respect. This is how true courage will emerge.

2. Let courtesy never fail

In the way of the warrior, courtesy is not simply a set of kind gestures or good manners. In reality, it is a virtue closely related to respect for the other, even if he is an enemy.

Courtesy is, above all, respect and consideration for the other, regardless of the circumstances. This means not being cruel or making unnecessary demonstrations of strength or power. It is a virtue that shows character and a lot of inner strength.

3. Compassion must always be present

The strength and power you have must be used for the good of all people. This is indicated by way of the warrior, who also insists on the enormous value of solidarity. This is a forcefully adorning feature.

Compassion is not just a feeling; it must be translated into concrete actions. Whenever someone can be helped, it should be done. And if you don't have the opportunity to help him, you have to find that possibility.

4. Justice above all

The way of the warrior says that justice has no half measures. According to this ancient wisdom, the just comes from defining what is right and differentiating it from what is not. The right is rewarded, and the wrong is punished.

To be fair is always to seek to act in the right way. This should not depend on what others say but on the person himself. Everyone knows in his heart what is fair and what is not. He must only follow that light that emanates from himself.

5. Loyalty is characteristic of strong and noble spirits

What you say or do belongs entirely to you. Therefore, the consequences are also ours. Hence, you must have a great sense of responsibility before acting or expressing yourself.

Loyalty is, above all, loyalty to oneself. Ability to be consistent or coherent. To that extent, it is also a commitment to answer for actions and words. Loyalty only belongs to the strongest and noblest.

6. The word and sincerity

For samurai, the word has immense value. It is not spoken by speaking, nor is it said by saying. So, on the warrior's path, words are equivalent to acts. When something is said, it is as if it was already done.

In this philosophy, the value of a promise is removed. This is not necessary. Suffice it to say that something will be done to commit to doing it. This is only possible for those who are completely honest with themselves and with others.

7. Honor exalts the human being

According to the warrior's path, the greatest virtue of all is an honor. Being honorable means acting upright, regardless of the circumstances. Fulfill duty and adhere to values, regardless of whether others approve this or not.

Honor is associated with self-respect. This implies not allowing yourself to fall into unethical or despicable behaviors. Honor is so important in this philosophy that if you lose, the only way to get it back is by taking your life.

The most interesting thing about the warrior's path is that being such an ancient ethical code, the values it promotes remain valid. The world would be very different if, in each conflict, or each confrontation, we applied those valuable principles of the samurai warriors.

CONCLUSION

How to manipulate and doing mind manipulation is a skill that is innate to each of us. Everybody is born with it. Each individual reacts and interacts with one another. That is how manipulation works in society. It brings people in and out. It is the way we communicate with one another.

How to manipulate is as important as how to communicate and relate to people. When we relate and convey our thoughts to our peers, we lure them into listening to us and understand our own beliefs if not agree to it. We base our success on how people respond to the thinking that we have. If we get favorable responses from people, we will feel satisfied, and that satisfaction builds up our whole being. If we somehow fail to be understood, we often resort to arguments because of our subconscious fights for the manipulative tactics of others. We do not want to be manipulated, but somehow, we tend to forget that every decision and actions that we take are only products of mind manipulation by others.

The saddest part is that we often fail to realize that we need to manipulate to survive and to be successful. If we only aim for survival, we don't need to practice a lot of mind manipulation techniques. But should we settle for less? We want to become more than and larger than ourselves.

The first thing we need to consider is that we need to understand that manipulation is not negative. Somehow, negative connotations impact the way we deal with people. We thought that being frank and direct about telling others our need is a kind of manipulation and, therefore, bad. We thought that when we ask someone to do the things our way it is a kind of manipulation, then we refrain from asking for help. We then fail to realize that we miss the chance to have a new door for an opportunity.

We take pride too much in ourselves about playing fair while the world is not. What we are trying to achieve, though, is not to trick everyone and mean them bad. We like to open our eyes to the opportunities that are just waiting to be unlocked. If we put up a cocktail party because we want to invite and be acquainted with somebody who we know can help us well with our interest, it is a kind of technique that we need.

Mind manipulation is within us. We do not need special psychic power to be able to manipulate people and be successful. We need to know the techniques and skillfully practice it.

www.ingramcontent.com/pod-product-compliance
Lightning Source LLC
Chambersburg PA
CBHW071814080526
44589CB00012B/790